Praise for

PRIDE

CELEBRATING DIVERSITY & COMMUNITY

AWARDS:

Stonewall Honor Book in Children's and Young Adult Literature

USBBY Outstanding International Books Winner

NOMINATIONS:

Bolen Books Children's Book Prize Shortlist

Hackmatack Children's Choice Book Shortlist

Information Book Award Shortlist

PNBA Book Award Shortlist

Rainbow Book List Commended

Red Cedar Book Award Shortlist

Red Maple Non-Fiction Shortlist

Rocky Mountain Book Award Shortlist

Sheila A. Egoff Children's Literature Prize Shortlist

"LGBTQ culture and rights are covered through the prism of Pride in this timely work...This attractive work will be welcomed by readers searching for guidance and hope."

—*Kirkus Reviews*

"Informative...Positively festive in its attitudes and outlook, this book more than lives up to the word celebrating in its subtitle."

—*Booklist*

"A visually appealing, quick, and thorough look at Pride parades and celebrations, how they came to be, and what they celebrate...An excellent and necessary addition for all collections."

—*School Library Journal*

"Upbeat and matter-of-fact...As useful and appealing as this book will be to a general audience, there will be another group of readers seeking it out with more focus."

—*Quill & Quire*

"Not only about celebration, but also protest and the future of acceptance... An eye-pleasing option for a broad audience and will lend itself to the conversation."

—*School Library Connection*

"A fantastic achievement, a book that gives serious attention to often ignored groups within LGBT history...Highly Recommended."

—*CM Magazine*

"This timely, attractive and cheerful book will engage any student from middle school and beyond...This book is a must-buy for all schools."

—*Resource Links*

"[*Pride*] does well to address the obstacles that the community has faced and puts names and faces to those who are the agents of change."

—*VOYA Magazine*

PRIDE

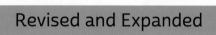

Revised and Expanded

PRIDE

THE CELEBRATION AND THE STRUGGLE

Revised and Expanded

Robin Stevenson

ORCA BOOK PUBLISHERS

Library and Archives Canada Cataloguing in Publication
Title: Pride : the celebration and the struggle / Robin Stevenson.
Names: Stevenson, Robin, 1968– author.
Description: Revised and expanded.
Identifiers: Canadiana (print) 20190180234 | Canadiana (ebook) 20190180242 | ISBN 9781459821248 (softcover) | ISBN 9781459821255 (PDF) | ISBN 9781459821262 (EPUB)
Subjects: LCSH: Gay Pride Day—Juvenile literature. | LCSH: Gay pride celebrations—Juvenile literature. | LCSH: Gay liberation movement—Juvenile literature.
Classification: LCC HQ76.5 .S74 2020 | DDC j306.76/6—DC23

The first edition of this book was previously published by Orca Book Publishers in 2016 (ISBN 9781459809932).

Library of Congress Control Number: 2019943980
Simultaneously published in Canada and the United States in 2020

Summary: This work of nonfiction for middle readers examines what—and why—gay, lesbian, bisexual and transgender people and their supporters celebrate on Pride Day every June.

Orca Book Publishers is committed to reducing the consumption of nonrenewable resources in the making of our books. We make every effort to use materials that support a sustainable future.

Orca Book Publishers gratefully acknowledges the support for its publishing programs provided by the following agencies: the Government of Canada, the Canada Council for the Arts and the Province of British Columbia through the BC Arts Council and the Book Publishing Tax Credit.

Edited by Sarah N. Harvey
Design by Rachel Page
Front cover photos by Norberto Cuenca/Getty Images and Perris Tumbao/Shutterstock.com
Back cover and flap photos by FG Trade/Getty Images, Perris Tumbao/Shutterstock.com, MAR Photography/Shutterstock.com, Nickolay Stanev/Shutterstock.com, DanielBendjy/iStock.com, Daphne Channa Horn/Shutterstock.com
Author photo: Stephanie Hull
Lyrics to "Rise Up" courtesy of Lorraine Segato/Lynne Fernie/Lauri Conger/ Steve Webster/Billy Bryans, Sony ATV Publishing

ORCA BOOK PUBLISHERS
orcabook.com

Printed and bound in China.

23 22 21 20 • 4 3 2 1

To my parents, Ilse and Giles; my partner, Cheryl; and my son, Kai, with love and gratitude. And to all the LGBTQ2IA+ kids and families out there—I wish you many happy Pride Days.

In memory of Kenneth Gerard Rogers (1954–1990)

CONTENTS

Celebrating Pride in Thessaloniki, Greece.
Giannis Papanikos /Shutterstock.com

INTRODUCTION

Every year, in many countries around the world, the LGBTQ+ community celebrates Pride Day. In big cities and in small towns, millions of people take to the streets to march in support of diversity, equality and freedom.

I went to my first Pride Day parade when I was still in high school. It was in Toronto, Ontario, in the late 1980s. These days, Toronto's Pride celebration is one of the biggest in the world, but back then it was much smaller. It felt huge to me though! I was enthralled by the beautifully decorated floats, the extravagant costumes and the music, and I was blown away by the sight of thousands of people dancing in the streets. I felt as if I had entered a magical world—one in which everyone could truly be themselves.

A group of people in New York City show their support for Pride. isogood/iStock.com

A small child watches the Pride parade in Victoria, BC. Tony Sprackett

I began attending Pride as a teenager because I had gay friends and I wanted to support them. A few years later, I came out myself and went right on attending Pride events as a proud member of the queer community. Now when I go to Pride, it is on the west coast of Canada, with my partner and our teenage son. He was only a month old at his first Pride Day! One of my favorite things about Pride is that it gives kids a chance to see that there are many kinds of families, and that all of our families are worth celebrating.

Pride Day is a spectacular and colorful event. But there is a whole lot more to Pride than rainbow flags and amazing outfits. Pride has a fascinating history—and it has always been a protest as well as a celebration.

So how did Pride begin? How is it celebrated, both here and all around the world? What does Pride mean to those who celebrate it? And just as importantly, what does it mean to those who cannot? Keep reading to find out—and to meet some of the many young *LGBTQ+* activists who are fighting to create a better world for all of us.

Celebrating Pride with my partner in Victoria, BC, in 2018. Kai Stevenson

A child waves a Pride flag during a Pride parade in London, England. Chris Harvey/Shutterstock.com

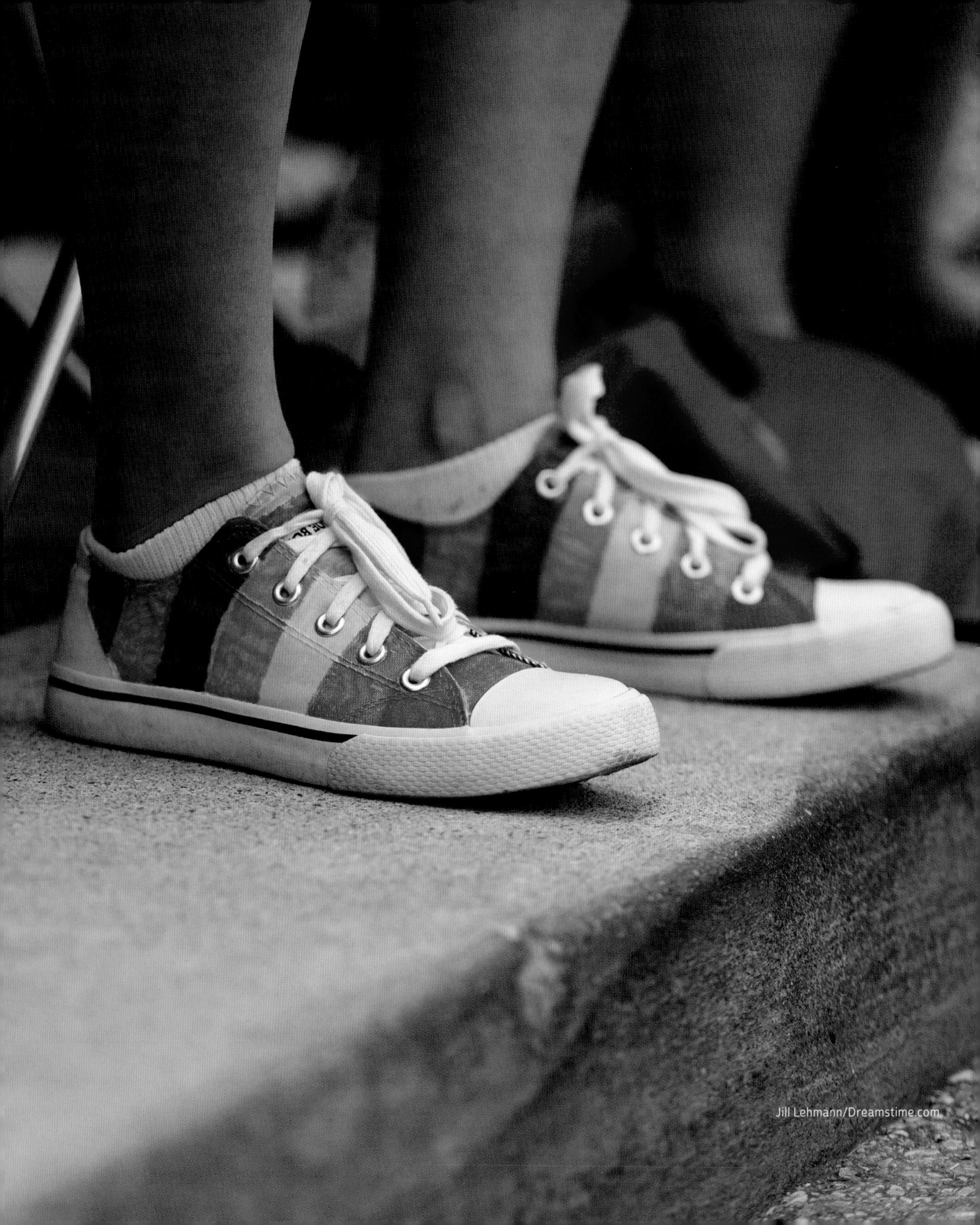

Jill Lehmann/Dreamstime.com

THE HISTORY OF PRIDE

IN THE BEGINNING

To understand the beginnings of Pride, you need to understand a bit of history. The world has not always been an easy place for men who love other men, women who love other women, and people who don't conform to traditional ideas about gender. In many ways, and in many parts of the world, this is still true—but here in North America, we really have come a long way.

Back in the 1950s, *lesbians*, *gay* men, *bisexuals* and *transgender* people (or *LGBT* people for short) did not have equal rights in Canada or the United States. It wasn't just that they couldn't get married—same-sex relationships were actually considered a crime! LGBT people didn't have legal protection from *discrimination*, so they could be evicted from their homes and fired from their jobs simply for being

Chicago Pride parade. Sianamira/Dreamstime.com

Activist Barbara Gittings, founder of the New York City chapter of the Daughters of Bilitis, picketing the White House in 1965.
Kay Tobin Lahusen/Wikipedia

who they were. Restaurants and bars could refuse to serve them. They could be arrested by police for being in gay bars or nightclubs, or for dancing with a same-sex partner.

But whenever there is **oppression**, there is resistance. People fight back—and that's how change happens.

FIGHTING BACK

One of the earliest gay organizations in the United States was the Mattachine Society, started in 1950 by a small group of gay men in Los Angeles. It was named for a group of masked medieval performers—a reference to the fact that gay men in the 1950s were forced to live behind masks, keeping their relationships secret. The men who joined the Mattachine Society in those early days also had another dangerous secret to keep: many of them had links to the Communist Party, and at that time, being a Communist could cost you your job—or even land you in jail.

A few years later, in 1955, two women called Del Martin and Phyllis Lyon gathered together eight lesbian women in San Francisco. They wanted a social group—and a place where the group could talk and dance together without risking arrest. Like members of the Mattachine Society, they had to be secretive, and most members didn't even use their real names. They called their organization the

QUEER FACT

IN 1972, ACTIVISTS BARBARA GITTINGS and Frank Kameny spoke to the American Psychiatric Association to help educate psychiatrists about homosexuality. Many doctors still believed that homosexuality was a mental illness, so Barbara and Frank asked Dr. John Fryer, a gay psychiatrist, to join them. He agreed—but the climate was still so hostile for LGBT people that he felt he had to disguise himself. He wore a mask and used a special microphone to alter his voice and was introduced as Dr. H. Anonymous.

Daughters of Bilitis, after a fictional lesbian character in an obscure poem. If anyone asked, they could say they were just a poetry club!

More groups began to form. Their memberships grew larger, and they became less secretive—and more political. In 1965, an activist named Craig Rodwell came up with an idea that led to some of the first public demonstrations by LGBT people: the Annual Reminders. Starting in July 1965, small groups of courageous activists picketed Philadelphia's Independence Hall each year, to remind Americans that LGBT people did not have basic civil rights. The first of these demonstrations had almost forty people marching, including members of the Mattachine Society and the Daughters of Bilitis. They carried signs to let everyone know what they wanted: *15 MILLION HOMOSEXUAL AMERICANS ASK FOR EQUALITY, OPPORTUNITY, DIGNITY.*

And momentum was building across the country. During the late 1960s, pickets and other protests also took place in New York, Washington, DC, Chicago, Los Angeles and San Francisco.

Gay rights demonstration in New York City, 1976.
Leffler, Warren K/Wikipedia

"Gay is Good" bumper sticker. DCVirago/Flickr

GAY IS GOOD

One of the early American civil rights activists who took part in the Annual Reminders was Frank Kameny. In 1957,

Frank Kameny attending Capital Pride in Washington, DC, in June 2010. The Pride parade route included a street recently renamed "Frank Kameny Way" in his honor. David/Flickr

"Justice triumphed. I was right, and they were wrong, and they admitted they were wrong."

—Frank Kameny

Kameny was fired from his government job for being gay. He was one of many Americans who lost their jobs during this era, because government officials thought gay and lesbian employees were vulnerable to blackmail by Communists. This fear, and the resulting **persecution** of thousands of gay men and lesbians during the 1950s and '60s, has been called the Lavender Scare. During this time, the Canadian government also attempted to identify and eliminate gay men and lesbians from the civil service, the military and the police force.

Frank Kameny decided not to accept this treatment, and he sued the US government in federal court. It was a battle that went on for eighteen years, through appeal after appeal, and it gained a huge amount of publicity for the growing gay rights movement. Ultimately, Frank Kameny lost the lawsuit—but he helped to win the larger battle for gay rights. He started a Washington, DC, chapter of the Mattachine Society and kept on fighting. In 1975, after a number of lawsuits, the government's anti-gay policy was finally changed. Today there are openly gay employees at every level of government.

Activists like Frank Kameny not only helped change policy, but they also fought to change attitudes. In the 1950s and '60s, many believed being gay or lesbian was a mental illness.

Activists argued against this idea, pointing out recent research published in two books called The Kinsey Reports. This groundbreaking research into a taboo subject showed that same-sex relationships were far more common than had previously been thought. Activists used the research in The Kinsey Reports as the basis for their statement that at least

My friends Khalilah and Katie at a Pride parade in Victoria, BC. Their T-shirts read *The first Gay Pride was a riot!*—a reference to the 1969 riots at the Stonewall Inn. Tony Sprackett

10 percent of the population was gay or lesbian—and this was very significant in helping to shift public opinion.

In 1960s America, a cultural movement known as "Black is Beautiful" was taking hold and challenging long-held racist ideas. Inspired by this, Frank Kameny coined the slogan "Gay is Good" in 1968. It was an attempt to counter the shame often felt by LGBT people living in such hostile times. "Gay is Good" was a move away from secrecy—and toward Pride.

HOW PRIDE DAY BEGAN WITH A RIOT

In the 1960s, there weren't many public places where LGBT people could gather. New York, which had one of the largest gay populations in North America, actually

> "... the Stonewall Rebellion was the shot heard round the world... The gay liberation movement was an idea whose time had come. The Stonewall Rebellion was crucial because it sounded the rally for the movement. It became an emblem for gay and lesbian power."
>
> —Lillian Faderman, historian and author of **Odd Girls and Twilight Lovers**

Stonewall Inn, site of the 1969 Stonewall Riots, New York City. On the window: *We homosexuals plead with our people to please help maintain peaceful and quiet conduct on the streets of the Village.*
—Mattachine
New York Public Library/Wikipedia

had a law that made it illegal for restaurants and bars to serve them. It was illegal for a man to dance with another man—or to wear clothing intended for the opposite sex! A woman could be arrested if she was wearing fewer than three pieces of "feminine clothing," and a man could be jailed for wearing a dress. Police regularly raided and shut down gay bars, arresting staff and customers.

One popular gay bar in New York was called the Stonewall Inn. It was on Christopher Street in Greenwich Village, and it was owned by the Mafia. The manager, known as Fat Tony, bribed the police with monthly payments so that they would turn a blind eye. It wasn't a fancy place—in fact, it didn't even have running water— but it was one of very few places where LGBT people could dance, chat, listen to music and be themselves.

Police raids weren't unusual at the Stonewall Inn, even with Fat Tony's bribes. Usually a few arrests were made. The bar shut down and reopened for business a few hours later. But on the evening of June 28, 1969, something was different.

QUEER FACT

THE STONEWALL RIOTS ARE FAMOUS—but not nearly as many people have heard of the Compton Cafeteria Riot. Three years before Stonewall, trans women and **drag queens** fought back against police harassment and brutality in San Francisco's Tenderloin district. Gene Compton's Cafeteria was a popular late-night hangout—but the management didn't like the drag queens and trans women who gathered there. They would call the police, who would clear the place out, arresting customers for "female impersonation." One night in August 1966, when a police officer grabbed a drag queen, she threw a cup of coffee in his face—and it was like throwing gasoline on a smoldering fire. People began throwing cutlery, flipping over tables and smashing windows. On the street outside, a crowd gathered, and dozens of people fought back as police forced them into paddy wagons. Amanda St. Jaymes is a transgender woman who lived nearby. "We just got tired of it," she said. "We got tired of being harassed. We got tired of being made to go into the men's room when we were dressed like women. We wanted our rights."

When the police arrested customers and began taking them to the paddy wagon, the crowd began to fight back.

As word of the demonstration spread throughout the city, the customers of the Stonewall Inn were soon joined by others from the gay, lesbian and transgender community. A crowd began to gather outside, shouting "Gay power" and throwing coins, bottles and bricks from a nearby construction site. It wasn't long before the police lost control of the situation and had to barricade themselves inside the bar.

Riot officers were called in wearing helmets with visors and armed with nightsticks and tear gas, but the crowd refused to give up. The conflict between the police and the protesters lasted until the early hours of the morning, and riots broke out again the next night, and the next.

The Stonewall Inn on June 24, 2016, the day President Barack Obama designated the Stonewall Inn and the land surrounding it as the first national monument dedicated to telling the story of the struggle for LGBT rights.
Drew Angerer/Getty Images

"Stonewall happens every day... When you go to a Pride March and you see people standing on the side of the road watching and then someone takes that first step off the curb to join the marchers, that's Stonewall all over again."

—Virginia M. Apuzzo, American LGBT rights activist and educator, former executive director of the National Lesbian and Gay Task Force, born 1941

PROUD MOMENTS

Sylvia Rivera (second from left) at the fourth annual Christopher Street Liberation Day March, 1973. The LGBT Community Center National History Archive/Richard C. Wandel

"I'm glad I was in the Stonewall Riot...that's when I saw the world change for me and my people. Of course, we still got a long way ahead of us."

—Sylvia Rivera, transgender activist and revolutionary (1951–2002)

I n many accounts of the Stonewall Riots, a transgender street kid called Sylvia Rivera is said to have thrown the first beer bottle at the police. But Sylvia Rivera's story doesn't begin or end with Stonewall. Sylvia was born as a boy, to Puerto Rican and Venezuelan parents, and raised in poverty by her grandmother. After conflicts related to her gender expression—she began wearing makeup in fourth grade—she left home to live on the streets at age ten. Poor, Latina, transgender and often homeless, Sylvia knew what it meant to be an outsider, and she spent her life fighting to make the world a better place for the most marginalized people in the LGBT community.

Sylvia was a founding member of the Gay Liberation Front and the Gay Activists Alliance, but as the gay rights movement became more mainstream, transgender people and drag queens often found themselves sidelined. Many activists seemed to focus on fitting in to the world, rather than changing it. Not Sylvia. A true revolutionary, she never stopped speaking her mind and fighting for the rights of street youth and transgender people of color.

One of Sylvia Rivera's closest friends was an African American transgender woman known as Marsha P. Johnson. Like Sylvia, Marsha had a difficult childhood, and she too found herself living on the streets at a young age. In fact, she and Sylvia met when they were both still in their teens. Marsha was six years older and often looked out for her younger friend. "Marsha would give the blouse off her back if you asked for it. She would give you her last dollar," Sylvia once said. Throughout her life, Marsha always spoke out against injustice. She was strong-willed and used to say that the *P* in her name stood for "Pay it no mind!"

Marsha was an important part of the community that fought back against the police during those nights of rioting at the Stonewall Inn. Shortly after that, she and Sylvia founded a group called STAR—Street Transvestite Action Revolutionaries—and they did everything from marching for change to helping create shelters for street kids.

Another person who played a significant role at Stonewall was a biracial lesbian called Stormé DeLarverie—a singer, bouncer, bodyguard and drag king who was born in New Orleans. She was one of several lesbians at the Stonewall Inn the night of the riots, and while accounts vary, some say that her fight with police was one of the events that spurred the crowd to revolt. She herself claimed to have thrown the first punch. Stormé said, "It was a rebellion, it was an uprising, it was a civil rights disobedience—it wasn't no damn riot." She continued to be involved in the gay liberation movement for many years after Stonewall and worked as a bouncer until the age of eighty-five.

Marsha P. Johnson at the fifth annual Christopher Street Liberation Day March in 1974. Leonard Fink Photographs/ The LGBT Community Center National History Archive

In the 1950s and '60s, Stormé DeLarverie performed as a drag king with a traveling variety show called the Jewel Box Revue. At that time, drag kings were called male impersonators. Stormé was the emcee and the only drag king in a cast of men performing as women. Photo courtesy of Lisa Cannistraci

Members of the Gay Activists Alliance carry a sign in a 1971 gay rights march in New York City.

Photo by Richard C. Wandel, courtesy LGBT Community Center National History Archive

AFTER STONEWALL

Lesbian, gay, bisexual and transgender people had fought back against the police before the Stonewall Riots, but not so fiercely and not in such large numbers. The Stonewall Riots became a symbol of resistance and changed the movement from a small group of activists to a much bigger fight for change. New groups were formed, including the Gay Liberation Front and the Gay Activists Alliance, and a month after the riots, the first mass rally for gay rights took place in New York City. It wasn't long before gay liberation marches began to spread across the country, the continent and the world.

Marches were an important part of all the social movements of the 1960s—the civil rights movement, the anti-war movement, the women's liberation movement and the youth liberation movement. It was a politically charged time. Activists who were organizing after Stonewall did not see gay rights as separate from other human rights issues. They saw connections between different forms of oppression, and they wanted to take action to make the world a better place for everyone.

QUEER FACT

THE POLICE RAID that set off the Stonewall Riots was led by Deputy Inspector Seymour Pine, on orders from his superiors. He later admitted that the police officers had held prejudices common at the time, and that in those days, raiding gay bars was seen as a good way for officers to boost their arrest records. He apologized for the raid in 2004, six years before his death at age ninety-one—and said that if his actions had, in the end, helped people by igniting the Stonewall Riots and the gay rights movement, then he was glad of that. In June 2019, fifty years after the Stonewall Riots, the commissioner of the New York Police Department publicly apologized to the LGBTQ+ community. "The actions and the laws were discriminatory and oppressive, and for that, I apologize," he said.

On June 28, 1970, one year after the Stonewall Riots, New York City had its first gay rights march.
Photo by Leonard Fink, courtesy LGBT Community Center National History Archive

Even though activists had been organizing for change for years, the Stonewall Riots are often seen as the beginning of the Pride movement. It was an important turning point for the community—so important, in fact, that people often refer to the 1950s and '60s as the pre-Stonewall era.

THE FIRST PRIDE PARADE

The first Pride parade was held a year after the Stonewall Riots, on June 28, 1970, although it wasn't yet called a Pride parade. Activists declared it Christopher Street Liberation Day and organized the first-ever gay rights march in New York City.

One of the organizers was Craig Rodwell, owner of the Oscar Wilde Memorial Bookshop on Christopher Street, the first gay bookshop in the country. Craig had been a member of the Mattachine Society, but he felt the organization was too conservative and that it was time for a

"We propose that a demonstration be held annually on the last Saturday in June in New York City to commemorate the 1969 spontaneous demonstrations on Christopher Street and this demonstration be called CHRISTOPHER STREET LIBERATION DAY."

—November 2, 1969, Craig Rodwell; his partner, Fred Sargeant; Ellen Broidy; and Linda Rhodes

A group of young activists at the 1970 gay rights march in New York City. Photo by Leonard Fink, courtesy LGBT Community Center National History Archive

bolder approach. The bookshop became a meeting place for a number of the newly formed activist groups, and its mailing list proved valuable in organizing the Christopher Street Liberation Day march. After much discussion, the group chose a slogan for the marchers to chant: "Say it clear, say it loud. Gay is good, gay is proud!"

That same weekend, marches were also held in Chicago, Los Angeles and San Francisco. The following year, Canada's first Gay Day Picnic was held in Toronto. By 1972, marches were being held in many cities across North America—and they were starting to pop up all over Europe too.

Many North American Pride events today are held on a weekend that falls close to June 28—the anniversary of the Stonewall Riots.

GROWING PAINS

Dropping the language of gay liberation and adopting the philosophy of gay pride represented a shift from protest

IN CANADA, AS IN THE UNITED STATES, the LGBTQ+ community was organizing for change. In 1971, a number of Canadian groups came together to write a document called "We Demand." Its 13 pages called for changes in laws and policy to end discrimination based on *sexual orientation*. On August 28, 1971, a week after "We Demand" was submitted to the federal government, more than a hundred people gathered on Ottawa's Parliament Hill in Canada's first lesbian and gay rights demonstration. People carried signs and chanted "Two, four, six, eight, gay is just as good as straight." Some people gave speeches. One was an activist named Charlie Hill, who said, "Throughout Canada's history, our sisters and brothers have been thrown into jail, hounded into hospitals, forced to hide... Even today, Canadian homosexuals are having their careers ruined, being kicked out of their churches, having their children taken away from them and being assaulted in the streets of their own cities." He went on to say, "Today marks a turning point in our history. No longer are we going to petition others to give us our rights. We're here to demand them as equal citizens on our own terms."

to celebration. Not everyone supported this change. Was Pride Day moving too far from its radical roots?

The LGBT community has always been diverse, and not everyone had the same political goals. Some people wanted to focus on the fight for the same rights that heterosexuals had, such as the right to marry. Others felt that we should embrace our differences from heterosexual, or straight, traditions, and that focusing on marriage equality was a mistake.

Another challenge to the growing Pride movement was the lack of **equality** within the community: **sexism**, **racism** and **classism** meant that while some voices were heard, others were silenced. Lesbians, who had fought alongside gay men from the beginning, were often invisible as male voices took center stage. Drag queens and people who

Gay Vietnam Vets protesting the war—and demanding equal rights—in a 1972 gay rights march. Photo by Leonard Fink, courtesy LGBT Community Center National History Archive

> *"It is not our differences that divide us. It is our inability to recognize, accept and celebrate those differences."*
>
> —*Audre Lorde, black lesbian feminist, poet and activist (1934-1992)*

A queer youth group marches in London's Pride parade.
Chris Harvey/Shutterstock.com

didn't conform to traditional gender roles were marginalized by those who thought they should try to fit in by appearing more like straight people. People of color and anti-racism activists challenged the community to address the racism within its ranks. People living in poverty, including LGBT youth whose parents kicked them out of their homes, faced different concerns than wealthy people. People with disabilities pointed out that meetings and events were regularly held in locations that weren't wheelchair accessible. Transgender people had long been a part of the community and had often led the way in fighting for change, but the violence and discrimination they faced were rarely made a priority by gay and lesbian activists. Although great progress has been made, all of these issues continue to be problems today.

Pride has had some growing pains, but the central values of diversity, equality and freedom have been a strong thread guiding the community through the decades of change. Still, just like any family, the community will probably continue to have its arguments.

That's part of how we learn—by challenging each other to grow.

YOUTH ON THE FRONT LINES

Young people were very active in all the social movements of the 1960s. Universities and college campuses were intensely political, with demonstrations and strikes being regular occurrences. Student activists protested against racism, against the Vietnam War, against sexism. They organized to work for peace, equality and social justice. So it is not surprising that young people have been involved in fighting for change since the earliest days of the gay rights movement.

The first high school-based LGBT activism started not long after the Stonewall Riots. In 1972, a group of students at New York City's George Washington High School got together and decided to organize for change. Most of them were people of color: they called themselves

People gather in front of the Stonewall Inn, in celebration of Pride, on June 28, 2019—the 50th anniversary of the Stonewall Riots.
Spencer Platt/Getty Images

QUEER FACT

IN 1976, THE YOUTH LIBERATION FRONT published a pamphlet called "Growing Up Gay." One of the anonymous teen authors called for youth to follow in the footsteps of the George Washington High School students, bringing political organizing into their schools. "Now it is up to us, the gay students, to have the courage to come out, so that we can help our gay brothers and sisters, as well as ourselves. If we demand the right to form our own groups, our self-pride, confidence, and self-respect will make life in high school much more bearable...We hold the future in our own hands."

Alberta teenager Carl Swanson started a GSA at his high school in Edmonton, AB. "I remember thinking that people my age pretty much spent their time in three places: at home, with their friends and at school," he said. "If I set up a GSA at my school, I could guarantee that one of those three places would be safe and welcoming for students like me." Ruby Swanson

In the early years of the AIDS epidemic, LGBT communities in North American cities organized politically to fight against AIDS, homophobia and government inaction. The first Fighting for Our Lives march was a candlelight march in New York City in 1983. Courtesy LGBT Community Center National History Archive

"Third World" students and they connected their activism with the gay liberation movement and with other civil rights struggles around the world. Soon other youth groups started to appear across the country, although most were less political: They focused more on providing support and connecting LGBT students and *allies*.

Today, thousands of schools across North America have groups that offer support for LGBT students and allies, and provide opportunities for them to meet each other. They also work to fight **homophobia** and **transphobia**, and to make school a safer space for all students. These groups are often called *GSA*s—which stands for Gay-Straight Alliances or, more inclusively, Gender and Sexuality Alliances. Others are called Queer-Straight Alliances, Pride Clubs, Rainbow Clubs—or, of course, whatever names

their members choose. (You can read more about school-based activism and young activists in chapter 5.)

SILENCE = DEATH

The first Pride Days I attended were in the late 1980s, at the height of the AIDS epidemic. Although we now know that anyone can get AIDS, the first people in North America to develop the illness were gay men. Young, healthy men were suddenly getting sick and dying—and no one knew why. It was a terrifying and devastating time for people in the gay community. Thousands had already died, and many more were ill. One of those men was my close friend and housemate, Kenny.

In the 1980s, little was known about AIDS. There were no effective treatments—but there was a great deal of fear and terrible prejudice. Several of my friends from university stopped coming to my house when they found out that I lived with someone who had AIDS. Some health care providers actually refused to treat AIDS patients.

By 1987, AIDS had spread to over a hundred countries—and more than twenty thousand people had died in the United States alone. And yet homophobia and indifference at the highest levels of government led to a shockingly inadequate official response.

But LGBT people and their supporters came together to fight for change. Using the slogan "Silence = Death," a small group of gay activists in New York challenged the LGBT community to turn their fear, their anger and their grief into action, and in 1987 a new group called ACT UP was formed. ACT UP (AIDS Coalition to Unleash Power)

"It will be recorded that the dead in the first decade of the calamity died of our indifference."

—Paul Monette (1945–1995), author of Borrowed Time: An AIDS Memoir

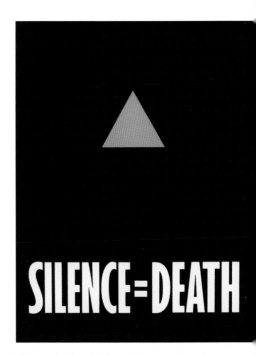

Silence = Death poster image. Wellcome Images/Wikipedia

The Second National March on Washington for Lesbian and Gay Rights took place on October 11, 1987, and half a million people took part. ACT UP, which had formed in NYC earlier that year, had a visible presence, which inspired participants from across the United States to form local ACT UP chapters when they returned home. Photo by Richard C. Wandel, courtesy LGBT Community Center National History Archive

and the LGBT community fought ignorance with education campaigns and fought discrimination in courtrooms across North America. They pressured governments, scientists and drug companies to do more research and to make new experimental treatments available.

These activists were hugely successful. In fact, they deserve much of the credit for the existence of medications that fight HIV (the virus that causes AIDS). These days, many people living with HIV can have long and healthy lives, as long as they have good access to treatment.

The AIDS epidemic is tragic. It devastated the gay community in the 1980s and '90s, and it continues to destroy millions of lives in many countries around the world. But the fight against AIDS made the North American LGBT community stronger, more politically organized and more visible—which set the stage for the next wave of activism.

THE QUEER NINETIES

In 1990, AIDS activists from ACT UP founded a new group: Queer Nation. Queer Nation was a response to the violence, harassment and prejudice that LGBT people continued to face, and its mission was to eliminate homophobia and increase LGBT visibility. Queer Nation's name represented the reclaiming of the word *queer*. Activists took back a word that had been used against them, as an insult, and proudly owned it: queer included anyone whose gender or sexuality fell outside what was narrowly considered to be "normal." And while not everyone in the community embraced the term, for the most part the reclaiming was a success: LGBT became LGBTQ+.

Queer Nation's tactics were direct and confrontational, and their message was clear: We're here, we're queer, and we're not going away! The group held "Nights Out," in which queer participants would go to straight bars and night clubs and dance with same-sex partners. Queer Nation took their activism beyond the cities and into the suburbs, organizing a Queer Shopping Network and traveling to malls to hand out flyers that read *We're here, we're queer, and we'd like to say hello!* The flyers included information about LGBTQ+ people and a list of famous queers throughout history.

Queer Nation logo by Alan MacDonald and Patrick Lilley from 1992. Wikipedia

Promotional material used by Queer Nation Houston. Wikipedia

Quebec couple Amy Stewart and Elena Abel got married in Nevada in 2015.
Trey Tomsik from Scenic Las Vegas Weddings

Ottawa couple Shelley Taylor and Natasha Coldevin.
Nathaniel Westley

In June of 1990, hundreds of Queer Nation members in New York City marched in the city's Gay Pride parade behind a banner that read *Queer Nation…Get Used To It!*

EQUAL FAMILIES, EQUAL RIGHTS

When I came out as queer in the early 1990s, lesbian and gay relationships were not recognized in Canadian law, and the *Canadian Human Rights Act* did not include protection from discrimination based on sexual orientation. But the fight against AIDS had politicized the LGBTQ+ community, and more and more gay, lesbian, bisexual and transgender people were living their lives openly, creating families and demanding recognition and protection.

I was living in Ontario at the time and involved with a local activist group. The provincial government was discussing a proposed new law called Bill 167, or the *Equality Rights Statute Amendment Act, 1994*. It was the first attempt to pass legislation recognizing our relationships in Canada, and if it passed, same-sex couples would have the same rights and obligations as heterosexual couples. It felt like we were on the verge of a historic victory.

We threw our energy into supporting Bill 167—organizing letter-writing campaigns, giving interviews on

QUEER FACT

IN 1985, FEWER THAN 25 PERCENT of Americans said that they had friends, relatives or colleagues who were gay or lesbian. By 2013, that number had risen to over 80 percent. These days, it is unusual NOT to know gay or lesbian people. The month before same-sex marriage was legalized across the country, a poll showed that the majority of Americans believed everyone should be able to marry. Young people were the most supportive, with nearly 8 in 10 saying they were in favor of same sex-marriage.

California couple Rachel and Susan Stewart got married in Sacramento in 2015. Allison Lal

local radio stations, putting up posters and holding public demonstrations. But when the members of the government finally voted, the bill was defeated. In Toronto, protesters filled the visitors' gallery in the legislature building, crying "Shame, shame!" before taking to the streets, where they blocked traffic and chanted, "We're here, we're queer, we all pay taxes."

At the time, I was devastated. How could anyone not see that our relationships—our families—needed recognition and protection? It was hard to accept that the government of my own country didn't think that we deserved the same rights everyone else had.

QUEER FACT

SOUTH AFRICA is the only country on the African continent to have legalized same-sex marriage, and it was the first African country to hold a Pride parade. The first South African Pride parade was held in Johannesburg on October 13, 1990, and events are held annually in a number of locations.

A group of marriage equality supporters with signs in front of the US Supreme Court Building in Washington, DC. Purdue9394/iStock.com

Bill 167 failed—but the LGBTQ+ community in the early 1990s really was on the verge of victory. The progress made in the years since that time has been remarkable.

In 2001, the Netherlands led the way, legalizing same-sex marriage. Belgium and Spain were quick to follow. In 2005, same-sex marriage was adopted in Canada. In the United States, recognition of same-sex marriage varied from state to state, so the battle for equality was fought on many fronts. Finally, in June 2015, a US Supreme Court ruling made same-sex marriage legal across the country.

QUEER FACT

PROGRESS RARELY FINDS A STEADY PATH forward, and there are often bumps and setbacks along the way. In February 2018, Bermuda became the first country to *repeal* marriage equality. The country had legalized same-sex marriage in the spring of 2017 only to reverse that decision less than a year later. Same-sex couples in Bermuda can enter into "domestic partnerships," which means they do have some legal protections, but they can no longer marry.

Same-sex marriage is now legal in more than twenty-five countries, including Canada, the United States, Mexico, the United Kingdom, Ireland, Germany, Denmark and many other European countries, as well as Argentina, Brazil, Colombia, Uruguay, Australia, New Zealand and South Africa. In May 2019, Taiwan became the first country in Asia to join this group—and a number of countries in Central America and South America are taking big steps toward marriage equality and seem likely to legalize same-sex marriage in the next few years. Other countries, such as Greece and Croatia, while not yet allowing same-sex marriage, have passed laws that give some same-sex couples many of the same rights as married couples.

Public opinion is just as important as legal change—and public opinion has also changed drastically. By *coming out* and living our lives openly, LGBTQ+ people have shown the world that we really are everywhere. And people generally don't hate or fear what they know. Support for LGBTQ+ rights is higher than it has ever been.

However, progress often provokes a backlash from those who fear change and hold on to old prejudices. In North America and around the world, the fight for LGBTQ+ equality and acceptance is far from over.

New York City Pride. Kobby Dagan/Shutterstock.com

A very young supporter gets a ride and waves a Pride flag in a Los Angeles Pride parade.
shalunts/Shutterstock.com

QUEER FACT

ON NOVEMBER 28, 2017, PRIME MINISTER Justin Trudeau stood in the House of Commons to deliver a historic apology to LGBTQ+ Canadians. He apologized for the decades of oppression, discrimination and injustice they had experienced at the hands of the Canadian government. To the civil servants, members of the military and all who had been treated as criminals because of their sexual orientation, he said, "You are professionals. You are patriots. And above all, you are innocent...It is our collective shame that you were so mistreated. And it is our collective shame that this apology took so long—many who suffered are no longer alive to hear these words. And for that we are truly sorry."

PROUD MOMENTS

PARENTS UNITE!

Jeanne Manford, founder of PFLAG, takes part in a 1974 Pride march with a group of other parents. Photo by Leonard Fink, courtesy LGBT Community Center National History Archive

Morty Manford knew he was gay from the time he was a teenager, and as a young man in New York City, he joined the Gay Activists Alliance. In 1972, while he was handing out leaflets to protest media oppression, Morty was attacked and beaten so badly that he was hospitalized for a week.

His mother, a schoolteacher named Jeanne Manford, was furious. "I'm very shy," she said. "I was not the type of person who belonged to organizations. But I wasn't going to let anybody walk over Morty."

She wrote a letter to the *New York Post*. "I mentioned that my son was gay and that the police stood by and watched these young gays being beaten up and did nothing." The letter was printed and soon everyone was talking about it. Jeanne was asked to be on a television show in Boston— and then in Cincinnati and New Orleans and Detroit. "I guess it was the first time a mother ever sat down and publicly said, 'Yes, I have a homosexual child.' I was never quiet about having a gay son. I'd tell strangers; I didn't care. I figured this was one way to educate people."

Later that year, Morty Manford asked his mother to march with him in the Christopher Street Liberation Day March. She agreed to join him—on one condition. "I'll march if you let me carry a sign," she told him.

She carried a sign that read *PARENTS OF GAYS: UNITE IN SUPPORT FOR OUR CHILDREN*. During the parade, Jeanne was amazed—and very moved—by the overwhelming emotional response of the crowd. People stood and applauded as she walked by, and many ran up to her, thanking her and hugging her. "As Morty and I walked along during that first march, we were talking about starting some kind of organization. So many people said, 'Talk to my parents,'" Jeanne recalled.

So Jeanne decided to start a support group for parents whose children were gay.

The first meeting was held at a church in New York's Greenwich Village. About twenty people came. And from that small group came PFLAG—Parents, Families and Friends of Lesbians and Gays. PFLAG went on to become a national organization that now has over 400 local chapters (or groups) and more than 200,000 members across the US. Using PFLAG's model, other countries have also started groups. PFLAG Canada has more than sixty local chapters! Australia, England, China, Israel, Italy, Vietnam and many other countries also have PFLAG groups.

Today, the sign that Jeanne Manford carried in the 1972 Pride parade is in the New York Public Library archives.

A parent marches in support of her gay son in a 1975 Pride march. Photo by Leonard Fink, courtesy LGBT Community Center National History Archive

"I felt that the love in my own home was more important than what others thought about me."

—Jeanne Manford, founder of PFLAG

Young and old, generations come together to celebrate diversity at a Pride Day picnic on Salt Spring Island, off the west coast of British Columbia. Flat Earth Photography

PRIDE AND IDENTITY

WHO GOES TO PRIDE EVENTS?

Pride is a celebration of diversity, equality and freedom—and everyone is welcome to enjoy it. The people who go to Pride Day parades and festivals include members of the queer community, their friends and family, people who support LGBTQ+ rights and believe in the importance of Pride celebrations, and many individuals and families who are looking for a fun and entertaining way to spend a day.

Seeing all the thousands of people supporting and celebrating Pride together was important to me when I first came out as queer. It helped me realize that I was not alone, that I was part of a large, vibrant and exciting community. Knowing that so many others were choosing

Three friends wait for the parade to pass by in Victoria, BC. Robin Stevenson

to be visible—to be open about who they were, to hold hands and dance together in the streets, to have fun and celebrate, to demand acceptance and respect, to fight for equal rights—helped me find the courage to do the same.

If you have never been to a Pride parade, you might not be sure what to expect. You might even be nervous—and that's okay, because it's all new to you, there are a lot of people, and it can be a bit overwhelming. Sometimes people worry about what others will say if they see them at a Pride event. That is understandable too, because we live in a world in which there is still a lot of ignorance and prejudice. It helps to go with a friend, if you can—and to keep in mind that you are welcome at Pride whether you identify as part of the LGBTQ+ community or are just there to show support. Do what is right for you—and if you do decide to go to Pride, bring a water bottle and some sunblock!

FINDING COMMUNITY

You have probably grown up with a number of cultural celebrations, events and holidays. They may be connected to your religion, like Passover or Christmas or Diwali, or to the country your ancestors came from, like Chinese New Year or Scotland's Hogmanay or Mexico's Dia de los Muertos (Day of the Dead). These celebrations are part of your cultural heritage, shared by your family and your community.

But while some aspects of identity—like culture, language and religion—are usually shared by all members of a family, others—like sexual orientation and gender

Celebrating Pride in Vancouver, BC. Tony Sprackett

identity —are often not. Pride Day makes the LGBTQ+ community more visible. And that is important, especially for young people who might otherwise feel very alone.

My friend Tom grew up in a small town in the Maritimes in the 1950s—long before the Stonewall Riots and the first Pride parades. By age ten or eleven, he knew he was different. He knew he liked boys, but he didn't know that anyone else in the world felt the same way. He didn't have any words for how he felt, and he couldn't imagine telling anyone. The only explanation he could think of was that he came from another planet. And every night he stared out his bedroom window, watching the sky and waiting for a spaceship to come and take him back to his own world. He was confused and desperately unhappy. A Pride parade—even if he didn't attend it, even if it wasn't

"When I was a teenager, I did the greatest activism I could ever do, which is to tell myself my truth and live that truth as an adult."
—Janet Mock, American writer, producer, director and transgender rights activist

Shutterstock.com

Celebrating EuroPride in Oslo, Norway.
Nanisimova/Shutterstock.com

Celebrating Pride in Orlando, FL.
Perris Tumbao/Shutterstock.com

in his town, even if he only heard about it or saw pictures in a newspaper—would have let him know that he was not alone. It would have let him know that people like him existed and could be happy and proud of who they were.

These days many young LGBTQ+ people all over the world find community on the internet. Online you can get information, ask questions, learn about LGBTQ+ identities and talk to others who share your experiences, without having to come out to anyone before you are ready. Of course, not all information online is accurate or helpful, and some teens experience homophobic or transphobic bullying on social media. Still, the internet is a tremendous resource, and young people now are much better

informed and less isolated than earlier generations of LGBTQ+ people.

WHAT IS "COMING OUT"?

Most heterosexual teens don't have to think too much about who they are attracted to or whether to tell their parents—and the majority of kids don't question whether they are a boy or a girl. For LGBTQ+ teens, though, this part of life is often more complicated. It is very common during the teen years, and sometimes much earlier, for questions about sexual orientation and *gender identity* to surface.

Coming out refers to the process LGBTQ+ people go through as they move toward understanding and accepting their gender identity or sexual orientation. It also refers to sharing that understanding with other people in their lives—for example, talking openly with their friends or family about their identity, their personal feelings or their romantic relationships. Coming out can be a gradual process, and many people choose to come out only to a few close friends at first. Some may be out to their online friends but not at school—or out at school but not at home. Others are comfortable being very open about who they are. Sometimes people aren't sure how they identify

"Navigating your teens is tough for anyone, but for someone who doesn't fall in line with society's expectations for sexual or gender identity, it can be extra difficult—even dangerous. Everyone has the right to be treated with dignity and respect, and we all deserve the space to explore our passions, pursue romance and present our real selves to the world free of judgment and aggression. The world is full of allies, friends and kindred spirits: find them, and with their support, let yourself shine."

—Tom Ryan, author of
Keep This to Yourself *and*
When You Get the Chance

QUEER FACT

OCTOBER 11 IS NATIONAL COMING OUT DAY, an annual holiday to celebrate coming out and to support LGBTQ+ people who have not yet done so. National Coming Out Day has been held every year since 1988. Why October 11? It is the anniversary of the 1987 National March on Washington for Lesbian and Gay Rights, a day on which half a million people marched on Washington, DC, in support of gay rights.

High school student Danny Charles is an Indigenous man who identifies as a female-to-male transgender person. He is a slam poet who loves to help out in his community, and he is working to make schools and foster care better places for LGBTQ+ youth.
Courtesy Danny Charles

"My advice would be to not compare yourself to anybody. You are amazing just the way you are. It's a long journey—but it is going to be fine."
—Danny Charles, British Columbia

or where they fit in. And sometimes people find that their identity shifts and changes over time. Everyone's experience is different, and that is okay.

Coming out is a very personal decision and one that no one should be pressured into making. It can be scary to come out to people, especially if you aren't sure how they will react. If you are too young to live independently and you suspect your parents will not be supportive, coming out to your family may be too risky. Happily, the world is changing, and while homophobic and transphobic attitudes are still a problem, they are gradually becoming less common. And there is a lot of support out there!

If you are thinking about coming out, or supporting a friend who is, there are some resources at the end of this book that you might find useful.

WHAT GROUPS MAKE UP THE QUEER COMMUNITY?

LGBTQQP2SIA…Help! Sometimes people joke about our community's ever-evolving attempt to name itself. And yes, it does look a bit like alphabet soup! One acronym you might see is *QUILTBAG*: Queer/*Questioning*, Undecided, *Intersex*, Lesbian, Transgender, Bisexual, *Asexual*, Gay/*Genderqueer*.

QUEER FACT

ARE YOU CISGENDER? If you've never really questioned your gender identity—if you and everyone else have just always taken it for granted that you are a boy or a girl—then you probably are. Cisgender refers to people whose gender identity matches the sex they are assigned at birth. For example, a cisgender woman is a woman who was identified as female at birth, has lived her life as female and sees herself as a woman. Because they are part of a majority, most cisgender people don't think much about their gender identity—and don't even know the word!

Proud to be trans! Salt Spring Island Pride parade. Flat Earth Photography

A shorter term that is sometimes used is GSM: Gender and Sexual Minorities. Another acronym you might see is SOGI. That one doesn't refer to the LGBTQ+ community: It just stands for sexual orientation and gender identity, which are two things that everyone has. Sexual orientation refers to which people you are attracted to, and gender identity refers to your internal experience of your gender.

When you have a community made up of people who have often been excluded or invisible, you want to create a space where everyone feels welcome, seen and included. So finding inclusive language is important. And, of course, language is always changing and evolving as people find or create new words to better describe their identities.

"I'm fighting for the abolition of apartheid. And I fight for the right of freedom of sexual orientation. These are inextricably linked with each other. I cannot be free as a black man if I am not free as a gay man."

—Simon Nkoli, speaking at South Africa's first Pride parade, Johannesburg, October 13, 1990

A group of Indigenous people drum their way through Vancouver's downtown streets in a Pride parade on Canada's west coast. Tony Sprackett

"The word 'queer' translates in Spanish to being 'rare.' But I don't like feeling as if I am an animal on the verge of extinction, so I have settled on 'lesbiana' in Spanish, because I want to honor in my native language my relationships with women. In English, I use the word 'queer.' It's a compromise. Words often are."

—Daisy Hernandez,
writer and editor

In this book, I often use the shorter version LGBTQ+ or just the word *queer*, which is an umbrella term often used to encompass all the people in our diverse community. I like it, and I refer to myself as queer—but not everyone in the LGBTQ+ community does. For some people, especially older gay men and lesbians who lived through less accepting times, the word is too strongly associated with memories of taunts, aggression and violence. For others, reclaiming and embracing the word for our own use is itself a sign of pride. So it is complicated. In general, it is best to refer to people using the language they choose to use for themselves. And if you aren't sure, ask!

LGBTQQP2SIA... UNDERSTANDING THE QUEER ALPHABET

Lesbians are women who are attracted to other women.

Gay refers to people who are attracted to members of the same sex. It is often used to refer specifically to gay men, but some women and non-binary people also identify as gay. Gay is also used more generally—for example, to refer to the gay rights movement.

B stands for **bisexual** (sometimes just called **bi**). Bisexuals are people who are attracted to two or more genders.

Transgender doesn't refer to sexual orientation (that's who you are attracted to) but to gender identity (your internal sense of being male, female or neither). The word **transgender** describes people who do not identify with the gender they were assigned when they were born. It includes people who were considered girls when they were born but who now identify as male, and people who were considered male at birth but now identify as female. It also includes people who don't fit into those categories at all—people who feel that they are neither male nor female or that their identity lies somewhere between or outside those categories. Some use the term **genderqueer** or **non-binary** instead of transgender. Some describe themselves as **agender**, **androgynous** or **gender non-conforming**. Others use the term **genderfluid** to describe a gender identity that shifts from day to day.

Q is for **queer**, a term sometimes used by LGBTQ+ people to refer to all those whose gender identity or sexual

Young people in colorful dresses and holding rainbow flags celebrate Pride in New York City.
Rommel Demano/Getty Images

New York City Pride march.
Kena Betancur/Getty Images

Sydney Mardi Gras Parade, Australia.
Jeffrey Feng

orientation falls outside the dominant heterosexual and gender-conforming mainstream. It also carries a political meaning—a challenge to the idea that heterosexuality and traditional gender identities are somehow "normal." People who identify as queer often emphasize the connections between different systems of oppression and the ways in which these systems reinforce each other.

Q can also be for **questioning**, which refers to people who may not currently identify as LGBTQ+ but are in the process of exploring and discovering their sexual orientation, gender identity or gender expression.

Pansexual people are those who are attracted to people of all genders.

2S, or sometimes just **2**, stands for **Two-Spirit**. This is a term used by some Indigenous people to refer to a person who has both a masculine and a feminine spirit. As a broad umbrella term, it can include a wide variety of Indigenous concepts of gender and sexual diversity. Many Indigenous Peoples have specific terms in their own languages that more accurately describe the social and spiritual roles of gender-variant members of their community. Historically, these individuals were often respected and highly valued.

Intersex people are those whose physical sex (their body, their chromosomes and their hormones) doesn't fit easily into traditional categories of male or female.

A stands for **asexual**. People who identify as asexual are generally not sexually attracted to anyone and feel little or no sexual desire.

An Indigenous marcher wears a traditional button blanket in a Pride parade in Vancouver, BC.
Tony Sprackett

"Two-spirited people are said to be gifted twice. We consider them very valuable people."
—Trudy Spiller, Gitxsan mother, grandmother and great-grandmother, Victoria, BC

BEING AN ALLY

We can all support struggles for equality and social justice—and we all should! As a white person, for example, I can take a stand against racism and act as an ally to people of color. Men and boys can be feminists and ally themselves with women and girls by challenging sexism and fighting for gender equality. And people who are not part of the LGBTQ+ community themselves can be allies in the fight for LGBTQ+ equality.

In fact, sometimes it is safer for people who are not part of a marginalized group to speak up. For example, as a cisgender woman, I could suggest that my workplace have an all-gender bathroom without fearing I would experience a backlash or be personally attacked for raising the issue. When we have privilege, we can and should use it to make our world better for everyone—and that is what being an ally is all about.

> *"Allying is what you do, not who you are. I've been moving away from calling people allies and instead talking about acts of allyship. It might sound like a little detail, but as a person who allies with other communities, it reminds me that the focus is on their needs, not my kindness. Alliance is an action, an allegiance, a commitment, but not an identity."*
>
> **–Alex Gino, genderqueer author of George and You Don't Know Everything, Jilly P!**

QUEER FACT

GENDER IS ABOUT HOW YOU FEEL, not about how you appear, so you can't really know what someone's gender is just by looking at them. Sometimes people will tell you what pronouns they use. For example, I use the pronouns she and her, so if you are talking about me, those are the pronouns you should use. And sometimes people might ask you what pronouns you use yourself.

For some people, especially those who identify as non-binary or genderqueer, neither *he* nor *she* feels like a good fit—so they may use *they/them* pronouns instead of *he/him* or *she/her*. It can take some effort to get accustomed to using new pronouns, but it's important—and it's not hard! In fact, you already use they as a singular pronoun in situations where you don't know someone's gender. For example, if you found a book left on a desk at school, you might say, "Hey, someone forgot their book. I hope they come back for it!"

It is important to use the correct pronouns. Using the wrong pronoun for someone—or "misgendering" them—can be very hurtful. Of course, we all make mistakes sometimes. If you accidentally use the wrong pronoun, just correct yourself and move on.

PFLAG members and supporters carrying messages of love and acceptance. Tony Sprackett

Nine-year-old Esme is making a Queer Pride T-shirt to show her support for the LGBTQ+ community.

Carrie Mac

Being an ally is really something you *do*, not something you *are*. It is about listening and learning—and it is about taking action and using your voice. A good place to start is by educating yourself. Learn about the language LGBTQ+ people use to describe their identities, and if this is all new to you, get comfortable saying those words. Listen to LGBTQ+ people who are sharing their feelings and experiences, take what they are saying seriously, and believe them—even when (*especially* when!) their experiences are different from your own. Stay open to learning. Remember that there are always LGBTQ+ people in every classroom, every workplace, every group, even if you don't know who they are and even if they are not out. You can

help them feel safer and more included by making sure everyone knows you support LGBTQ+ people. Even small, simple things—like wearing a rainbow button—can send a powerful message.

And if you see something happening that isn't okay, speak up! We can all do that, whether or not we are a part of the community most directly hurt by it.

PFLAG: PARENTS AS ALLIES

One group of allies that is very visible in many Pride parades is PFLAG, an organization that provides support for families, allies and people who are LGBTQ+, and also engages in education and advocacy to bring about full equality. My parents started a PFLAG group because they wanted to support the fight for equal rights. My mother, Ilse, remembers: "I first walked in a Pride parade in Toronto in 1992. My daughter had come out the year before, and I wanted to support her. I was somewhat unsure how it would be, not being much of a parade kind of person, but it was one of the most overwhelming experiences of my life. As the group of parents walked by, the noise of the crowd watching us grew to a roar: shouts and whistles, and people of all ages rushing up to give us hugs, saying, 'Thank you, thank you!' I had no idea that the support of a group of parents would mean so much."

My mother, Ilse, hands out PFLAG flyers at a Pride parade in Toronto in the mid-1990s.
Robin Stevenson

My parents, Giles and Ilse, hanging out with my sleepy, face-painted three-year-old at Victoria's Pride Festival in 2007. Robin Stevenson

QUEER FACT

PHOENIX, ARIZONA, is home to Native PFLAG—the only PFLAG chapter in the US that focuses on supporting Native American LGBTQ+ and Two-Spirit people, their families and friends. In 2019, the chapter hosted its first Two Spirit Powwow, with dancers from across the country.

Amanda Saenz is a Latinx, queer, non-binary intersex activist and educator. In 2015 they made history by becoming the first intersex person to portray an intersex character in a TV show.

Photo by Emily Quinn

> *"Your lives matter, your voices matter, your stories matter."*
>
> -Laverne Cox, American actor and trangender rights activist

> *"I think being gay is a blessing, and it's something I am thankful for every single day... I couldn't be more proud of being gay."*
>
> —Anderson Cooper, American journalist and author

LADIES AND GENTLEMEN, BOYS AND GIRLS...

Our society likes to classify people, and one of the most basic categories that we structure our society around is sex. Male and female. Men and women. Boys and girls.

But it isn't really that simple. Some people are non-binary: their gender identity is neither male nor female. And other are intersex: they are born with anatomy, hormones or chromosomes that don't fit neatly into the categories of male or female. For example, a person may be chromosomally male, with XY chromosomes, but their physical development may appear typically female because of an insensitivity to male hormones. Or a person may be born with mosaic genetics, so that some of their cells have XX (female) chromosomes and some of them have XY (male) chromosomes. Being intersex is not as rare as you might think. In fact, it is about as common as having red hair.

Until quite recently, doctors usually assigned a sex to intersex babies—deciding for them whether they would be raised as male or female. Often doctors operated on babies to make their genitalia conform to the gender they had been assigned. Parents were advised not to tell anyone about their child's condition, and the children themselves were usually kept in the dark about their medical history and the procedures performed on them.

In more recent years, intersex adults have spoken out against these practices and the shame and secrecy that resulted from them. They have organized to work for change, and some have allied themselves with the LGBTQ+ community. Being intersex is a physical condition, not a sexual orientation or a gender identity, but like gay, lesbian, bisexual and transgender people, intersex people face oppression based on sexism, homophobia and the idea that there are only two genders. It makes sense to come together to fight for a world in which all those who live outside traditional sex and gender norms can freely express themselves and be proud of who they are.

Intersex activist and educator Emily Quinn works to raise awareness about intersex people. "When I present to students, doctors and even the general public," she says, "my main point is that intersex people don't need to be fixed. There's nothing wrong with us, and we don't need to be operated on in order to lead happy and healthy lives." She also points out that while our society likes to put people into boxes labeled male and female, the reality is much more complicated. Thousands of intersex babies are born every year, and millions of intersex people exist around the world. "So there's a lot of us," she says. "We're not new or rare. We're just invisible. We've existed throughout every culture in history. Yet we never talk about it."

But thanks to intersex people who are speaking up, those conversations are starting to happen.

"Pride is an opportunity: it creates a space where people come together to not only celebrate the progress made in LGBT+ politics, but also to learn about the histories of the diverse identities that Pride celebrates by creating a safe environment that naturally fosters healthy discussion...Being intersex is something that I have come to accept and cherish about myself. To see so much positivity flying around when people talk about intersexuality only makes me more hopeful for the future because it means that things are getting better."

—Amanda Saenz

Intersex activist and educator Emily Quinn gives a TED talk to raise awareness about intersex people. Marla Aufmuth & TED

PROUD MOMENTS

Me, age twenty-two. Robin Stevenson

MY COMING-OUT STORY

I didn't come out as a teenager. I had a few friends who were gay, but I didn't start to question my own sexual orientation until after I graduated from high school, spent a couple of years at university and went to Australia to work. I was twenty-one. I got a job at a university cafeteria and spent lots of time looking after horses and riding along gum-tree-lined trails in the South Australia heat.

I also thought a lot about my past relationships and what I wanted in the future. I broke up with my boyfriend. And I started dating women.

After I returned to Canada, I came out to my parents and my friends. For a few years I said I was a lesbian. Later, I started identifying as bisexual—or as queer. I wasn't always sure what word fit best, but one thing I was sure about was that I did not want to hide who I was—or who I loved—from the people that mattered to me.

I was lucky. My parents, my brother and sister and most of my friends were open-minded and **queer-positive** individuals who have always supported me completely.

Sadly, not everyone is met with the kind of support that I received. I have friends whose coming out was met with anger, judgment and even rejection from the people they loved.

Coming out is a process that never really ends. All these years later, I still have to come out to people regularly. But why is my sexual orientation anyone's business?

Here's the thing: Being queer isn't just about my sexual orientation—it's about my life! I am coming out when I introduce people to my family. I'm coming out when my partner and I hold hands in public. I'm coming out when I explain that my son doesn't have a dad, he has two mothers. I'm coming out every time I talk about my partner.

Because we live in a culture that tends to assume people are heterosexual unless they say otherwise, hetero-sexual or "straight" people don't have to come out.

My mother and her friend Irene co-founded PFLAG Hamilton in the early 1990s to provide information and support to other parents of LGBTQ+ kids, and to advocate for equal rights.
Robin Stevenson

At Toronto's Pride parade in the early 1990s.
Robin Stevenson

PROUD MOMENTS

COMING OUT IN HIGH SCHOOL

Duncan Smith, playing piano at home in Ontario.
Heather Smith

Duncan Smith is a gay teen who lives in Ontario. He came out at a much younger age than I did. "I first began questioning my sexuality when I was around twelve or thirteen," he told me. "It was around that age when I started to realize that I was 'different.' However, I didn't 'officially' come out until about fourteen."

Duncan began by talking to one person he trusted. "I started out by telling my closest friend," he said. "That was the first time I openly spoke about my sexuality. It felt good to finally be open about that aspect of myself, so, naturally, I wanted to share with a few more close friends and family members. Next I told my parents, which was probably the hardest thing to do. But it went wonderfully; both were very positive and understanding! It was relieving, but not at all surprising: my parents are both accepting, loving people. That was probably my best experience."

Outside his family, Duncan did encounter some homophobic attitudes. "There were a few less-than-satisfactory reactions from a couple of friends, particularly those with highly religious views," he recalled. "One friend even went so far as to suggest that homosexuality is caused by a 'birth defect.'" Still, he counts himself lucky, as the people who mattered most to him were very supportive.

Duncan said he isn't a huge fan of labels. "I identify as gay—not for myself, as I am happy to be me. I don't need to be confined within a label," he explained. "I apply this label to my sexuality because it seems to make things easier for others to understand. My sexuality doesn't define me, but it is a part of me which has shaped who I am as a person."

He has thought a lot about the concept of Pride. "For me, Pride is the ability to love another human being without shame, feeling comfortable in your own skin, and not having to hide your true self," Duncan said. "Pride is about embracing your uniqueness. Nobody should be ashamed to be different. Rather, it is something to be celebrated. It's also important to recognize that there isn't just one way to be 'gay'—being gay isn't a particular lifestyle, appearance or set of values or tastes. So Pride can be about celebrating one's differentness, even from other LGBTQ+ people. Within this community there is lots of diversity. Everyone expresses themselves in a unique way—this is what makes our community beautiful and worthy of Pride!"

> *"Pride comes in many different forms; everybody shows their pride in different ways. The expression of pride is just as diverse as the community itself."*
> —Duncan Smith, age 17, Waterloo, ON

QUEER FACT

ALTHOUGH MANY LGBTQ+ TEENS are happy, confident and surrounded by supportive friends and family, some are not. LGBTQ+ youth are more likely to experience bullying, harassment and even violence. They are more than twice as likely to attempt suicide. And LGBTQ+ youth whose families do not accept them face an increased risk of homelessness.

Parents, family members and friends can make a big difference by listening, being supportive, respecting teens' choices and privacy, educating themselves about LGBTQ+ issues and publicly supporting equal rights. And schools can help too. Teachers play an important role in creating safe school environments that value diversity and support all students. They can encourage student-led support groups such as GSAs, and they can help make sure students have access to counseling and resources.

PROUD MOMENTS

FIGHTING FOR FAIRNESS

Harriette Cunningham proudly shows her new birth certificate. Sandy Aitken

Harriette Cunningham is a transgender girl who lives with her family on Vancouver Island. When she was born, everyone thought she was a boy—but she never felt like one. As a young child, Harriette wanted to grow her hair long and wear dresses. Some boys like to wear dresses too, but for Harriette it wasn't just about clothes. "I've always known I was a girl, even when I was considered to be a boy," she explained. "In my dreams I was never a boy."

As Harriette got older, she had to help her parents see who she really was—not their son, but their daughter. Once they understood that she was transgender, they supported her 100 percent.

Harriette has a strong sense of justice, and it didn't seem fair that even after she changed her name and started living as a girl, her birth certificate still said she was a boy. It caused practical problems too: whenever she signed up for sports or traveled to the United States to visit her grandmother, she had to show a document that inevitably caused questions and confusion.

So when Harriette was ten, her parents and her grandmother decided they would fight for the right to change her birth certificate to reflect her gender identity. They wrote dozens of letters to the provincial government. When the legislation in the province was finally changed, in 2014, Harriette was eleven years old. She was one of the first—and the youngest—in line to get her new birth certificate.

Harriette's birth certificate was a victory, but she didn't stop there. She joined other activists in lobbying the provincial government for better protection from discrimination based on gender identity and gender expression—a battle that was won when protections for transgender people were added to the BC Human Rights Code in 2016. Harriette also filed a human rights complaint arguing that gender designation should be removed from birth certificates altogether. "So when a child is born, they won't label it," Harriette said. "If that had happened for me, it would've been a whole lot easier." In Canada and the United States, many activists are now fighting to get gender designation taken off not just birth certificates but all government-issued identity documents, such as driver's licenses and passports. Gender-free ID would make life much easier for many people!

"Pride is celebrating who you are and being true to who you are."
—Harriette Cunningham, Comox, BC

Harriette with her little brother, three-year-old Khosi. Sandy Aitken

Pride parade in Milan, Italy.
Eugenio Marongiu/Shutterstock.com

3

CELEBRATING PRIDE TODAY

WHAT HAPPENS ON PRIDE DAY?

Pride Day is a celebration of diversity and equality, a day when everyone can express who they truly are. In many places, Pride Day has grown into Pride Week—or Pride Month—and that takes a lot of organizing! Many cities have large planning committees that work hard to organize a variety of activities leading up to Pride Day. Every celebration is a little bit different, and each community adds its own flavor to the festivities, but most Pride celebrations include a parade and a festival, and a number of other events.

People of all ages take part in New York City's Pride march. Erika Cross/Shutterstock.com

Two children carry a Pride flag in Vancouver's Pride parade. Tony Sprackett

PRIDE PARADES

The Pride parade is the highlight of most Pride Day celebrations. Pride parades range in size from a few dozen people to hundreds of thousands. Some are relatively quiet and low-key, while others are lavishly extravagant productions. The parades often include floats—gorgeously decorated trucks playing music and loaded with people dancing.

Many groups and organizations march in Pride parades, usually carrying banners to show who they are and what they represent. Some of the groups you might see represented in a Pride parade include community organizations, libraries, food banks, schools, churches and synagogues, unions, political parties and local businesses.

Others march on their own or with family or friends. A Pride parade can be a very social event, with people

running into acquaintances and stopping to chat along the way. Some years I walk in the parade with other queer families, and some years my partner, my son and I sit on the sidelines and watch the parade. My parents usually come and watch too. We often see people at Pride whom we haven't seen for months! For many families, Pride is a fun day out.

DRESSING UP FOR PRIDE

For lots of people, a Pride parade is a chance to dress up, to get in touch with their inner performer and to strut their stuff. It's a time to get out the highest heels, the wildest wigs, the longest eyelashes, the brightest feather boas. Of course, the streets are also full of people in T-shirts and shorts—but

Pride parades and festivals make a fun day out for families and people of all ages. Tony Sprackett

My friends Lindsay, Dea and their toddler Zinnian celebrate Pride as part of a group of queer farmers. They handed out bunches of rainbow chard all along the Pride parade route! Robin Stevenson

Dykes on Bikes lead the way at the start of many Pride parades. Tony Sprackett

many pictures of Pride parades show people wearing elaborate, colorful, sometimes over-the-top costumes.

When I first came out, I wasn't completely comfortable with this aspect of Pride parades. I was pretty shy, and the last thing I wanted to do was draw attention to myself. I worried that people would see a few pictures of a Pride parade and think that LGBTQ+ people wear outrageous costumes all the time. Pink wigs! Sparkly tutus! Fairy wings!

Duncan, the Ontario teenager you met in the last chapter, shared a similar reaction. "I've attended a St. John's Pride parade in Newfoundland. Personally, I'm not into those sort of events—it's a little too much for me. I find them loud and a bit 'in your face,'" he told me. "As an introverted gay person, I want people to know that being gay does not mean that I am necessarily a flamboyant and over-the-top individual."

Of course, the LGBTQ+ community is made up of all kinds of people—and no particular image can ever represent us all. For most people, the way they dress in the Pride parade isn't the way they dress every day. That fellow in the sequined dress and high heels, dancing on the float? He might wear jeans to his day job at the garden center. And the leather-clad woman on the motorbike, with the rainbow-collared rottweiler riding on the back? She looks different in her gray suit when she defends clients in a courtroom.

Dressing up can be a lot of fun, but there is more to it than that. In the first chapter of this book you read about how LGBTQ+ people used to be arrested for wearing clothing that crossed traditional gender lines—sometimes called cross-dressing—and you learned about the important role drag queens, transgender and gender nonconforming people played at Stonewall and throughout LGBTQ+ history. Today, queer people who don't conform to traditional ideas about gender are more likely to be harassed and even beaten up. Boys who wear makeup and girls who wear suits to the prom often don't have an easy time in school. There is a lot of pressure to fit in. But at Pride, everyone has the space to safely express

At Pride, people celebrate their freedom to express themselves by dressing however they choose. Some people wear beautiful and elaborate costumes.
Tony Sprackett

"Pride is a time to celebrate the diversity, resilience and beauty of the queer community."
—Amanda Littauer, author, historian, mother

QUEER FACT

DYKES ON BIKES is a lesbian motorcycle club whose members often lead Pride parades. This tradition began in a San Francisco Pride parade in 1976, and all these years later, it is still going strong.

Two men walk hand in hand in a
Pride parade in Oslo, Norway.
Nanisimova/Shutterstock.com

themselves and wear whatever they like—and to celebrate their freedom to do so.

I still tend to wear my regular clothes to Pride—plus a rainbow flag or two—but these days one of my favorite things about the parade is seeing the incredibly imaginative, artistic and stunningly gorgeous costumes that some people wear. The Pride parade is a showcase of the creative spirit and the diverse beauty of the LGBTQ+ community—and I am very proud to be a part of it.

THE POLITICS OF PRIDE

Pride Day is a celebration, and sometimes it feels like a great big party…but its roots are strongly political. Coming out and openly living our lives and identifying ourselves as part of the queer community is, in itself, a powerful and political act, and one that has led to a great deal of change. Being visible is important—and thousands of people in a parade are definitely visible!

But the politics of Pride are complicated. The LGBTQ+ community is diverse, and many people within it experience multiple forms of oppression. For example, a Black teenage boy who comes out as a young gay man faces not just homophobia but also racism. Queer people who have disabilities have to deal with false assumptions, prejudice and discrimination. Racism, sexism, *ableism*—these are complex systems that intersect and reinforce each other. For Pride to truly represent all LGBTQ+ people, Pride events need to take a stand against not just homophobia and transphobia but against all forms of oppression.

In a Pride parade, many people march to bring awareness to a particular issue. If you read the signs and banners

Maia (top) and Violet celebrating Pride on Salt Spring Island. "I think it is cool to just be yourself. I feel like some people have to give up some friends to have their freedom, but I think it is worth it to be yourself... And I guess when I go to a Pride parade, that's really what I'm supporting." —Maia Jen MacLellan

Pride parades and Pride marches are about political activism as well as celebration. Participants make their communities visible, demand equal rights, and stand up for social justice. Tony Sprackett

Ten thousand people came out to support the tenth annual Norwich Pride parade, in the U.K.! Some watched the Parade from in front of the historic Guildhall.
Shutterstock.com/ Mary Doggett

being carried by marchers, you will get a glimpse of some of the political battles that are being fought. *Support our LGBTQ+ Seniors! Queers Against Racism! Fight Transphobia! People With Disabilities: Also Here, Also Queer!*

Community and school-based LGBTQ+ youth groups are often visible in Pride parades. Queer kids and teens are coming out at younger ages, which in many ways is a good thing—it shows that more young people are accepting themselves and realizing that it is okay to be open about who they are. On the other hand, if their families and peers are not supportive, LGBTQ+ youth can be at high risk for bullying, rejection and even homelessness. Helping LGBTQ+ youth who are facing problems at school and at home is an important priority for advocacy groups.

FESTIVALS AND POST-PARADE PARTIES

Pride parade routes are often planned to end at a park, where the parade turns into a great big party often called a Pride festival or post-parade party. In New York City, the Pride march goes right by the Stonewall Inn and ends in Greenwich Village, where it all began. Pride festivals usually feature a stage with live music and entertainment, dancing, food trucks and vendors selling everything from ice cream to rainbow hats and ties. Marchers, spectators and the general public are welcome to join in. It's a great time to catch up with friends and soak up the atmosphere.

Pride festivals often include a special kid-friendly zone, with entertainment geared to children and families. In Toronto, Family Pride runs all weekend long, offering snacks, music, games and crafts. San Francisco has an

Most Pride festivals include some activities for kids—like fabulous face painting! Robin Stevenson

LGBTQ+ Family Garden, with a playground and plenty of activities, special LGBTQ+ Family Days at local museums and even a Pride Kids Fun Run. The festival my family goes to is much smaller than the ones in bigger cities—but it still has a children's area with bouncy castles, face painting, Hula-Hoops and craft stations.

OTHER PRIDE WEEK EVENTS

In many cities, Pride Day comes at the end of a week or even a month of special events. Pride events can include concerts, drag shows, roller derby, baseball, fundraising runs, film festivals, theatrical productions, dances, beach parties and more.

I love seeing families celebrating Pride together. As this dad's T-shirt says: Respect the right to be different. Robin Stevenson

Puppy Pride! This handsome fellow is enjoying the sunshine and the sea breeze at Victoria's annual Big Gay Dog Walk. Robin Stevenson

As a writer and book lover, one of my favorite local Pride events is Pride in the Word, an evening of readings by LGBTQ+ poets and writers. There really is something for everyone. Victoria's Pride Week even has an event for queer dog owners: The Big Gay Dog Walk!

SYMBOLS OF PRIDE: RAINBOW FLAGS AND PINK TRIANGLES

If you go to a Pride parade or a Pride festival, you will see a lot of rainbows.

Why all the rainbows? It goes back to 1978, when artist and activist Gilbert Baker designed a rainbow flag as a symbol of pride and diversity, and flew it at San Francisco's Pride Day. And it definitely makes for colorful celebrations!

In addition to the rainbow flag, there are a number of other flags that represent specific groups within the

At a Pride parade in Delhi, India. abhishek jain/Gettyimages

LGBTQ+ community. The trans flag is light-blue, pink and white. It was designed by transgender activist and US Navy veteran Monica Helms and made its official debut at a Pride parade in Phoenix, Arizona, in the year 2000. She explained that the pink represents trans women, the blue stripe represents trans men, and the white stripe represents non-binary people. The bisexual flag is pink, purple and blue; the pansexual flag is pink, yellow and blue. The non-binary flag is yellow, white, purple and black; it was designed in 2014 by seventeen-year-old Kye Rowan, who chose colors not associated with traditional ideas of gender as binary. In 2017, the City of Philadelphia added black and brown stripes to their flag to show the inclusion of people of color, and some other cities have followed in their footsteps. And in 2018 a Portland designer named Daniel

Marchers at a Pride parade in Mariehamn, Finland, carry the rainbow flag and the trans Pride flag.
Arthur Lomarainen/Shutterstock.com

Non-binary flag

Progress flag

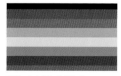

Philadelphia Pride flag

Each year in June, San Francisco's City Hall is lit with rainbow colors in celebration of Pride.
Nickolay Stanev/Shutterstock.com

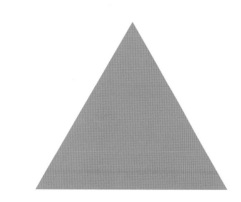

A child celebrates Pride at the New York City Pride march.
Steve Edreff/Shutterstock.com

Quasar created a new design he called the Progress flag. It combines the rainbow flag and, in an arrow at the side, the colors of the trans flag along with stripes of black and brown. The arrow indicates both forward movement and the progress that still needs to be made. As the community evolves, so will our ways of representing it.

Another symbol you might notice on T-shirts, signs and banners is the pink triangle. It has a disturbing origin: in the concentration camps of Nazi Germany during World War II, all prisoners were forced to wear a badge identifying them. Jews wore the yellow star. Gay men wore the pink triangle. Thousands of gay men were imprisoned in Nazi concentration camps, and many of them died. In the 1970s, the gay community reclaimed the pink triangle, originally intended as a badge of shame, and turned it into a symbol of Pride.

Other symbols you might see at a Pride event include the *labrys*, a double-headed ax from ancient Crete, which represents lesbian and feminist strength, and the *lambda*, a Greek letter used in many countries as a symbol of gay and lesbian community. The lambda was adopted as the international symbol for gay and lesbian rights by the International Gay Rights Congress in Scotland in 1974. The Lambda Literary Awards (affectionately known as the Lammies) are given out each year to recognize and honor the best new LGBTQ+ books and writers. The lambda and

the labrys aren't as visible as all the rainbow flags, but if you look for them at a Pride festival, you'll probably find a few! They are often used on signs, T-shirts and jewelry.

Three teens in Victoria, BC, wearing (from left to right) the pansexual Pride flag, the transgender Pride flag and the rainbow Pride flag.
Robin Stevenson

PERFORMING GENDER: THE ART OF DRAG

Many Pride parades and festivals include drag shows—performances by drag queens, drag kings and other drag artists. Traditionally, drag queens are men who dress in an exaggeratedly feminine fashion, with heavy makeup, glamorous dresses and high heels. Drag kings are usually women who dress as men or perform typically male roles—for example, doing a stage show lip-synching songs by male singers. Non-binary people can be drag artists too,

Labrys
Shutterstock.com

Lambda
Shutterstock.com

It's drag queens versus drag kings in Victoria Pride's annual drag ball game.
Victoria Pride Society/PBJ Photography

"Anyone can wear a dress—male, female, or anyone in between! I am a guy. I love performing as female characters on the stage in front of crowds of people. Doing drag allows me to become any character I can imagine! Drag allows me to bring some extra sparkle and smiles to my and other people's lives and that's why I do it. I do drag because I love how it makes me and others feel!" —Ryan, aka Dixie Paul Chappel

playing with gender expression and challenging traditional ideas about gender—and sometimes about drag itself—in diverse and creative ways. For many drag artists, drag is about performance and self-expression. It is hard to generalize when it comes to drag performers and drag culture, because there are many different kinds of drag, but one thing is for sure: drag has been a part of gay culture in Western countries for a very long time, and Pride wouldn't be the same without it.

FAMILY PRIDE

For many families, Pride Day is an important annual celebration. The first time I took my son to Pride Day, he was one month old—and, of course, he slept through most of it! We have been many times since then. As a parent, one of the things I like about Pride is that kids are able to see that families come in an infinite variety of configurations—that there are many different kinds of families to celebrate. There are single-parent families. There are families with two moms and families with two dads. There are blended families, families with step-parents, families formed through divorce and remarriage. There are families with transgender parents. Some families are formed through adoption. Some gay men create families with the help of a surrogate mother. Some queer woman conceive with the help of sperm donors.

And, of course, you don't have to have kids to be a family. Some LGBTQ+ people consider their closest friends to be another kind of family—a chosen family.

At Pride, it's okay to be all of who you are. One of the songs that is often played at North American Pride festivals is "We Are Family"—and at Pride, that's usually how I feel.

"Drag for me is the thing that helps me express myself. You get to be super creative; you can add your taste in dance, add your flavor. You can be sassy, you can be fierce, you can be whatever you want to be. You can be a magical fairy-tale creature, you can be a favorite character, you can just be a regular dude or a fabulous queen, whatever you want. Queen or King or Thing, everyone is included. Drag is the best thing that ever happened to me because I joined a new community of support and love. I've made great friends. Drag makes me feel included." —Alex, eleven-year-old Canadian drag artist and activist Lauren Sortome

A family participates in the San Francisco Pride parade. kobbydagan /iStock.com

PROUD MOMENTS

MAKING A FAMILY

From left to right: Biff, Hailey, Riley and Trystan.
Kevin Truong

Families come in all shapes and sizes and get made in many different ways. Here is one family's story.

Riley, Hailey and baby Leo live in Portland, Oregon, with their dads, Trystan Angel Reese and Biff Chaplow. As a family, they like to cook, play games, go on adventure walks and watch movies. Hailey likes *Star Wars* and fashion, and Riley likes soccer.

Back in 2012, Biff and Trystan were a young gay couple living in Los Angeles, with no thoughts of having children. They became parents suddenly and unexpectedly: Biff's sister was unable to care for her young kids, so Biff and Trystan decided to take the leap and adopt them. Riley was three years old, and Hailey only one. Biff and Trystan had an instant family.

It took a little while for the kids to settle because they'd had a difficult start in life, and Trystan and Biff had to adjust to a whole new life as parents. But by the time Riley and Hailey were in elementary school, everyone was happy and thriving. So Trystan and Biff decided to add a new family member by having a baby.

For most gay male couples, of course, getting pregnant isn't an option. But Trystan is a transgender man. He was raised as a girl but realized as a teen that he was trans, and a few years later he **transitioned** to living as a man. He took hormones, which gave him a beard and a deeper voice, but he still had all the parts he needed to make a baby—ovaries to make eggs and a uterus to carry a growing fetus. Trystan explained, "I think that what we're doing is what queers have always done, which is taking the pieces that are given to us and making something beautiful out of it." Many other transgender men have become parents this way.

With their doctor's support, Trystan and Biff were able to conceive. Nine months later, Trystan gave birth to a beautiful, happy baby. They named the baby Leo. Riley and Hailey were excited to meet Leo, though they hadn't been sure they would enjoy having a baby in the house. "Don't babies cry a lot?!" they asked their dads. But it turned out Leo was pretty calm and loved being their little brother. Hailey reads to him every day, and Riley can't wait for him to be old enough to play catch.

When Leo goes to Portland Pride with his family, he will see hundreds of happy people and lots of beautiful colors as they march in the parade. And other people in the community will see Leo and his family and know that anyone can find love and build a family if they choose to.

Trystan and Biff with baby Leo. Erin Schedler

"Because of homophobia, it isn't always easy to feel proud. But remembering that we are connected to the original Stonewall rebellion—that we are part of a sacred lineage of rabble-rousers and rioters—can remind us that we are people who see possibility where others see barriers."

—Trystan Angel Reese, social justice activist and educator

Muslims for Progressive Values supporting LGBTQ+ rights in a Pride parade in Columbus, Ohio.
Picklesaddie /Dreamstime.com

These teachers from Ontario's Catholic schools waved rainbow flags as they marched in Toronto's Pride parade.
Shutterstock.com/Shawn Goldberg

PRIDE AND RELIGION

Of course, your sexual orientation and gender identity are only part of who you are. We all have many different aspects to our identities, and for a lot of people, one important part of who they are is their religion. Jewish, Protestant, Muslim, Catholic, Hindu, Wiccan, Buddhist…there are LGBTQ+ people within every religious tradition.

Historically, much opposition to LGBTQ+ rights has come from religious organizations, and for LGBTQ+ people who have a strong religious identity, this conflict often causes emotional pain and self-doubt. It can make coming out more difficult and can lead to difficulties with family members. In some cases, coming out leads to rejection by one's religious community.

And yet, within every religious tradition there are strong voices calling for acceptance, for equality, for change. More and more religious organizations are welcoming LGBTQ+ people and standing up for equality, and some now recognize same-sex marriages. Many inclusive churches, synagogues, mosques and faith-based organizations show their support of LGBTQ+ people by participating in Pride parades and festivals.

QUEER FACT

HOMOPHOBIA is the fear or hatred of people who are gay, lesbian or bisexual.

HETEROSEXISM is a system of beliefs and attitudes based on the idea that everyone is or should be attracted to the opposite sex. This system of belief leads to prejudice and discrimination against LGBTQ+ people.

TRANSPHOBIA is the fear or hatred of people who are transgender.

CISSEXISM is the system of beliefs based on the idea that gender is binary (only male or female) and that all baby boys will grow up to be men, and all baby girls will grow up to be women. These beliefs ignore the existence of trans and intersex people, deny that their identities are valid and lead to their oppression.

Pride parade and festival in Brighton, England.
Photo by Tristan Fewings/Getty Images

The group Universalist Muslims, which describes itself as "queer affirming," works for human rights and has a visible presence in Pride parades. Shahla Khan Salter, one of the founders of Universalist Muslims, said, "We marched because we believe Allah loves us all—queer and straight, cis and trans; because we believe trans and queer Muslims enriched Islamic history for centuries…We marched to send a message to others to not lose hope, and so that one day they may join us."

"I felt deeply grateful to be part of something where I felt like I was letting people know in a very public way that they were loved," said Rabbi Shoshanah Conover of Temple Sholom, about marching in Chicago's Pride parade. "It felt good to me that collectively here we are in this huge parade, all of us together, to show this openness and welcoming. It was truly pride."

In Copenhagen, Denmark, Jewish marchers carry a rainbow flag with the Star of David on it.
Flemming Hansen/iStock.com

Pride parade in Copenhagen, Denmark.
oleschwander / Shutterstock.com

CONTROVERSY, CHALLENGE AND CHANGE

In recent years the LGBTQ+ community has made huge progress. In Canada, our legal rights are protected, and same-sex relationships are increasingly accepted. In the United States, the election of Donald Trump began a period of backlash and painful setbacks, but this does not erase the tremendous work that has been done over the past half century. There are still battles to be fought, but while we fight those battles, we can also celebrate the fact that LGBTQ+ people are able to live more openly than at any time in history.

As LGBTQ+ people became more visible, politicians began attending Pride parades to show support—and seek votes. Businesses recognized that Pride Day was an opportunity for them to promote their products and services. Banks, taxi and tourism companies, restaurants, bars and nightclubs all began decorating floats and joining

San Francisco Pride.
MindStorm/Shutterstock.com

QUEER FACT

ONE CONTROVERSY OFTEN in the media in recent years involves the presence of police officers at Pride parades. Should they be allowed to march, in uniform, alongside the LGBTQ+ community?

The relationship between police and the LGBTQ+ community has a long and troubled history that goes back to police targeting gay establishments, the police raids that triggered the riots at Compton's Cafeteria and at Stonewall, and the police harassing and arresting people for many years before—and since—that time.

Some in the LGBTQ+ community have argued that the police have come a long way since those days. They see police as protecting the community and consider their presence at Pride marches a sign of progress. But others have pointed out that for Black people, Indigenous people and other people of color, as well as for many transgender people, uniformed police may represent not protection but danger—and their presence can make Pride events feel less welcoming and less safe.

At the same time as New York's Stonewall 50 celebration, activists held a Queer Liberation march—a political march to highlight the struggles of the most marginalized members of the community. It included moments of silence for those lost to homophobia, transphobia, racism, and violence—and a die-in, organized by ACT UP, to honor the HIV+ asylum seekers who have died in ICE custody.
Kena Betancur/Getty Images

New York City's Dyke March—not a parade, but a protest against discrimination, harassment and violence. a katz/Shutterstock.com

the parades. While being seen as potential customers is certainly an improvement over being refused service, many people in the LGBTQ+ community dislike the increasing commercialization and consumerism of Pride Day celebrations.

Others feel that Pride events don't represent them. Transgender people, people of color, people with disabilities, Two-Spirit people and others have argued that their lives and identities are marginalized within the LGBTQ+ community and within Pride celebrations. Pride parades tend to be so dominated by white, cisgender, able-bodied gay men that other identities become invisible.

Many large cities hold *dyke marches* as part of Pride Week. Dyke marches are not parades. They are political demonstrations organized to increase visibility for lesbians and transgender people and all women who love women,

however they identify themselves. In the last few years, *trans marches* have also become part of many Pride celebrations, with the goal of increasing visibility, awareness and support for transgender people.

Some communities hold alternative Pride marches. These are usually grassroots political events that strive to challenge racism, colonialism and transphobia, embrace the full diversity of LGBTQ+ people by making transgender, Two Spirit and other marginalized identities more visible, and provide a non-commercial alternative to Pride. Dyke marches, trans marches and alternative Pride marches are often wonderful events, celebrating some of the many identities and communities that make up the larger queer community, but it is important to recognize why they have become necessary and work toward making all Pride events more inclusive.

In May 2016, Canada's government introduced a new law to protect transgender people from discrimination. A few weeks later, Toronto held its eighth annual Trans March, and a record-breaking number of transgender people and allies showed up in support. Thousands of people filled the streets, with Black Lives Matter Toronto leading the march. (The new law, known as Bill C-16, was passed and took effect a year later, during Pride month in 2019.)

THE CANADIAN PRESS/Eduardo Lima

People drive golf carts in the first Pride parade held on Protection Island, BC, a small community of about three hundred people off Canada's west coast.
Wendy Martin

NOT JUST FOR BIG CITIES

Pride is continuing to grow! In small towns across Canada and the United States, more and more communities are deciding to hold their own Pride events. It isn't always easy. When Steinbach, Manitoba—a conservative religious town of thirteen thousand—planned its first Pride parade in 2016, all but one member of the city council announced that they would not attend. But in an incredible show of support, five thousand people showed up, coming from as far away as Vancouver, Toronto and Orlando. Traffic was backed up for twelve miles (twenty kilometers) on the highway into town! Young LGBTQ+ activist Mika Schellenberg, who was seventeen at the time, said, "Steinbach Pride means being able to be who I am in a town where that wasn't always the case. It sends a message to those who aren't out yet that there are people just like them in Steinbach, and in other rural communities."

In 2018, in Owen Sound, Ontario, a queer sixteen-year-old called Ryan Brown organized his community's first Pride parade. "A parade sends a message," he explained.

"That message is sent to other queer people who haven't come out yet, telling them there is a community waiting for them, and it is sent to the people who have come out and have faced discrimination based on their identity. Pride events show that no matter the hardships, bullying, inequalities and oppression LGBTQ+ people have faced and continue to face, we are together as one community of people. It is important to remember that everyone deserves to be themselves unapologetically, and Pride events are a great reminder."

American teenager Erin Bailey also organized her community's first Pride parade in 2018—in Columbus, Indiana, the hometown of US vice president Mike Pence. "If you can make a difference right where you live, it still helps make a difference in the world on a larger scale too," she said.

High school senior Erin Bailey organized the first-ever Pride festival in Columbus, Indiana—and more than two thousand people attended!
Photo by Tony Vasquez

A crowd gathers in front of the Colosseum during a Pride parade in Rome, Italy.
alessandro0770/iStock.com

PRIDE AROUND THE WORLD

FIGHTING FOR FREEDOM AND EQUALITY AROUND THE WORLD

For many people, Pride is a celebration—but it is important not to let the rainbows and parades mask the ongoing struggles that LGBTQ+ people still face. There is no federal law protecting LGBTQ+ people from discrimination in the United States, and in more than half of the states, people can still be fired for their sexual orientation. Transgender people have even less protection: in more than thirty states, it is legal to fire someone solely because they are transgender. Not all families are supportive, and some queer teens are even kicked out of their homes by families that don't accept who they are. Hate crimes and acts of violence toward LGBTQ+ people

At the London, UK, Pride parade, a marcher lifts a sign demanding trans rights. In England, North America and around the world, trans people continue to face harassment, discrimination and violence.
Bikeworldtravel/Shutterstock.com

> *"I am an American, but like many of our LGBTQ brothers and sisters around the world, I consider myself to be a world citizen and a member of one human family."*
>
> —Gilbert Baker, designer of the rainbow flag, speaking at the 2007 InterPride conference in Zurich, Switzerland

In October 2018, hundreds of people gathered in Philadelphia's Love Park to protest the Trump administration's attacks on transgender rights.
Rachael Warriner/Shutterstock.com

still happen, and transgender people and queer people of color are most at risk. All of these things make it hard for LGBTQ+ people to feel safe.

In recent years the US government under the Trump–Pence administration has tried to undo some of the progress that has been made—it has banned transgender people from serving in the military, argued that discrimination against LGBTQ+ people should be allowed, cancelled policies that helped to protect trans students in schools, denied visas for same-sex partners of diplomats and appointed judges who have a history of not supporting LGBTQ+ equality.

In some parts of the world, LGBTQ+ people are still fighting for the most basic of rights—the right to be who they are without fear of violence or imprisonment. There are many places where being openly gay or lesbian is very dangerous. Same-sex relationships are still illegal in over seventy countries, most of them in Africa, the Middle East and Asia. In a few of those countries, individuals in such relationships can be punished with the death penalty. In many others, people can be arrested and imprisoned.

Anti-gay laws are one of the legacies of colonialism. In Africa, for example, same-sex relationships are illegal in more than thirty of the continent's fifty-four countries. And yet, prior to the European colonization of the continent, many traditional African cultures accepted diverse sexualities and gender identities. Worldwide, over half of the countries that criminalize same-sex relationships are former British colonies. (For more information on colonial laws, see the Queer Fact on page 119.)

London Pride. jgolby/Shutterstock.com

In Eastern Europe, same-sex relationships are not against the law, but they are not legally recognized either. Same-sex marriage is not allowed. Discrimination and violence against LGBTQ+ people are common in many Eastern European countries, and some of these countries have even introduced laws that limit free speech by banning what they call "gay propaganda," which includes all Pride celebrations and any efforts to protect or promote LGBTQ+ rights.

Some countries are taking steps to move toward equality, but others seem to be slipping further and further away from it. In the last few years a number of countries have introduced harsh new anti-gay laws.

Despite these risks, LGBTQ+ people around the world continue to fight for their rights. As Duncan Smith,

"I appeal to all governments and societies ... to build a world where no one has to be afraid because of their sexual orientation or gender identity."

—UN Secretary-General António Guterres

In 2014, World Pride was held in Toronto, ON.
mikecphoto/Shutterstock.com,

the teen whose coming-out story you read in chapter 2, said, "LGBT equality is when everybody, regardless of their sexual or gender identity, is treated as equal. This is not achieved until everybody on our planet Earth can feel safe about expressing their sexual orientation."

GOING GLOBAL: WORLD PRIDE

World Pride, as its name suggests, is an international celebration of LGBTQ+ Pride. It is organized by InterPride, an organization that is made up of Pride coordinators from around the world. InterPride chooses the city where World Pride events will be held, and selects a theme for that year's festivities. World Pride festivals, which are usually several years apart, include at least a week of art, sports and social events leading up to the World Pride parade. Rome hosted

"It is an outrage that, in our modern world, so many countries continue to criminalize people simply for loving another human being of the same sex...Laws rooted in nineteenth-century prejudices are fueling twenty-first-century hate."

—Former United Nations Secretary-General Ban Ki-moon

the first World Pride event in 2000, followed by Jerusalem and London.

In 2014, World Pride was held in North America for the first time, and the host city was Toronto, Ontario. The theme for this fourth World Pride was Rise Up, and the Canadian band Parachute Club released a new remix of its iconic song "Rise Up" just in time for the ten-day-long celebration. Events included an international human rights conference, an exhibition marking the forty-fifth anniversary of Stonewall and ten open-air stages featuring performances by numerous musicians and artists. The weekend-long street fair featured a kid-friendly Family Pride space, with activities and entertainment geared to children and families.

"We want power, we want to make it okay,
Want to be singing at the end of the day,
Children to breathe a new life,
We want freedom to love who we please..."

—From "Rise Up," by the Parachute Club

The Pride parade in Rome, Italy, draws many thousands of people. Lucky Team Studio/ Shutterstock.com

In London, the annual Black Pride UK celebration promotes unity among LGBTQ+ people of African, Asian, Caribbean, Middle Eastern and Latin American descent. Bikeworldtravel/Shutterstock

London Pride. Manyukhina/Dreamstime.com

Toronto's World Pride also included three marches—the Trans March, the Dyke March and the World Pride Parade. All were well attended, with the World Pride Parade setting a record for duration—it lasted over five hours! Over two hundred elaborately decorated floats sailed by, thousands of people marched, and many tens of thousands more watched the parade.

Toronto buses and crosswalks were painted with rainbow stripes, the CN Tower was lit up with rainbow lights, Niagara Falls shone with the colors of Pride. And over a hundred same-sex couples—some of whom traveled from other countries, including Australia, Scotland and Taiwan—tied the knot in a Grand Pride Wedding!

In 2017, World Pride was celebrated in Madrid, Spain. It marked the fortieth anniversary of Spain's first Pride parade back in 1977. More than a million people lined the streets of the Spanish capital, and many more took part in related events, including hundreds of thousands of people who had traveled from other countries, booking almost every hotel room in the city! The slogan for World Pride Madrid was "Whoever you love, Madrid loves you."

In 2019, World Pride returned to North America. It was held in New York City, where more than four million people attended a parade to celebrate the fiftieth anniversary of the Stonewall uprising.

The New York City Pride march passes the Stonewall Inn as it winds through through Greenwich Village.
lazyllama/Shutterstock.com

Madrid City Hall and the Cibeles Fountain lit in the colors of the rainbow for World Pride 2017.
Javitouh/Getty Images

In 2019, almost 100,000 people attended the Pride parade in Helsinki, Finland. Subodh Agnihotri/Getty Images

EUROPE

Europe's annual Pride celebration is called EuroPride, and it has a longer history than World Pride. It began in 1992 and is an annual event hosted by a different European city each year. EuroPride has been held in many spectacular locations, including Berlin, Stockholm, London, Warsaw, Copenhagen, Rome, Marseille, Vienna, Amsterdam, Zurich and Madrid.

Many European countries celebrate Pride with parades, film festivals, concerts and other events. Austria's capital city, Vienna, decorates its trams with rainbow flags for the month leading up to its Pride parade. Germany boasts huge parades in both Cologne and Berlin, as well as many smaller ones across the country, and France has

In England, beside the River Thames, the London Eye is lit in rainbow colors for Pride.
Pajor Pawel/Shutterstock.com

Pride parades in at least twenty different cities. The United Kingdom holds several large Pride events, with the biggest being in London and Brighton. London also hosts Black Pride UK, to celebrate and promote unity among LGBTQ+ people of African, Asian, Caribbean, Middle Eastern and Latin American descent. And Amsterdam hosts Canal Pride—a Pride parade held on boats in the city's canals.

In Eastern Europe, the social climate and laws are less supportive of Pride. Some Eastern European countries have not yet held Pride events, and in others Pride parades have been marked by violent protests, clashes between marchers and anti-gay protesters, injuries and arrests.

AUSTRALIA

Australia's largest and most famous Pride festival is the month-long Sydney Mardi Gras, which attracts hundreds of thousands of people from all around the world. It takes place in February and March—summertime in Australia— and includes a parade, numerous parties, concerts and performances, a queer film festival, art shows and a number of sports events, from runs to cycling tours to bowling nights. For families, Victoria Park is a great place to go for Fair Day, with international food, market stalls, rides, comedy, dance, live music—and even the famous DoggyWood dog show!

All these events lead up to the Sydney Mardi Gras Parade. About ten thousand people take part, many riding on fantastic floats or dressed in elaborate costumes. Fireworks are launched from the rooftops of buildings along the parade route, and hundreds of thousands of

A child rides a scooter in the Sydney Mardi Gras Parade. Jeffrey Feng

"I think a few years from now we're going to look back and wonder how homophobia was ever acceptable."

—Imran Khan, actor

Children clap and dance during the Mardi Gras Parade in Sydney, Australia. Hamid Mousa

A big smile on the face of this young marcher in the Sydney Mardi Gras Parade! Hamid Mousa

spectators line the streets to cheer and show their support as the parade goes by.

For many years, LGBTQ+ people in Australia have been fighting for marriage equality. In December 2017 they won that battle, and Australia became the twenty-fifth country to recognize same-sex marriage. And in June 2018 the Sydney Mardi Gras celebrated not only that important victory but also its own anniversary: forty years of passion, pride and protest.

SOUTH AMERICA

From São Paulo, Brazil, to small towns along the Amazon River, South America is home to some of the world's largest Pride celebrations, as well as some of its most remote ones.

In São Paulo, the entire month of June is Pride Month, and people come from all over the world to celebrate. Brazil has a large and vibrant LGBTQ+ community, and the country has recognized same-sex marriage since 2013. But a new president took power in early 2019, and many are worried about what his extremely homophobic and transphobic views will mean for their community—and for future Pride celebrations in Brazil.

Brazil's neighbor, Argentina, is also supportive of LGBTQ+ rights and hosts Pride events that attract many thousands of people.

Also in Brazil, but at the other end of the scale in terms of size, is the small Amazon town of Benjamin Constant, which held its first Pride celebration in 2011. Benjamin Constant is located right at a three-way border with Colombia and Peru, where the Amazon and Javari Rivers intersect. A town of about thirty thousand people, it has a diverse and religious community, little wealth, but abundant local fruit and fish. Benjamin Constant's first Pride celebration included a day-long forum discussing LGBT+ education, health and security issues, followed by a parade with more than sixty people marching through town, carrying a large rainbow flag. The song "I Will Survive" was played, and a supportive crowd followed along, dancing or riding motorbikes, chanting slogans and honking horns as they made their way down to the port.

Celebrating Pride in São Paulo, Brazil.
MAR Photography/Shutterstock.com

QUEER FACT

SOUTH AMERICA'S largest Pride parade is in São Paulo, Brazil. In 2006 it made it into the Guinness Book of World Records as the biggest Pride parade in the world. There is only one event in São Paulo that is bigger than Pride Day: Formula One racing!

Supporters hold a banner in Iquitos, Peru: *Regional March Against Transphobia.* Gart van Gennip

Other South American countries, like Peru, have lagged behind when it comes to LGBTQ+ rights, with discrimination and prejudice being common. But change is happening, and young people are more supportive of LGBTQ+ rights than older generations have been. Some government officials have predicted that same-sex marriage will soon be legalized in the country. Lima, Peru, hosts a small Pride event. Its claim to fame is that it is run by what is possibly the oldest LGBT rights organization in Latin America; the Movimiento Homosexual de Lima (Homosexual Movement of Lima) was established in 1982.

In the meantime, Peruvians continue to celebrate Pride. Iquitos, an isolated jungle town in the Peruvian rain forest that is inaccessible by road, holds an annual Pride parade. "Even in the poorest neighborhoods, people are completely

Pride supporters hold a sign in Iquitos: *Homosexuality is not a disease. Homophobia is.* Gart van Gennip

accepted members of the community, and they are able to live the way they want, without fear," one resident told me. About two hundred people take part in the Iquitos Pride parade, either marching or watching the festivities.

Two gay men at a Pride parade in Seoul, South Korea. Samuel Murray

SOUTH KOREA

The Seoul Queer Culture Festival in South Korea includes a Pride parade that is one of the largest in Asia. It was first held in the year 2000, and about fifty people attended, many of them hiding their faces to protect their identities. Every year the festival has grown, and now tens of thousands of people march, and tens of thousands more show up to watch, to celebrate and to show support.

Despite this, the LGBTQ+ community in South Korea is still much less visible than it is in North America and Europe. Discrimination is not uncommon. In 2014, the

Protesters tried to block this Pride parade in Seoul, South Korea, but the LGBTQ+ community and its supporters persisted.

Samuel Murray

Pride parade was brought to a complete standstill when conservative Christian protesters lay in the streets to block the parade route. But the marchers refused to give up. They stayed in the streets, kept blasting their music and kept dancing on top of the parade floats—for five hours! A huge white-and-red banner reading *Love conquers Hate* flew above the crowd. Finally, determined to finish the parade, the leaders took it on an unplanned route that avoided the protesters. The following year the parade was cancelled when officials refused to give a permit to the organizers. But the LGBTQ+ community didn't give up, and Pride parades have been held successfully every year since then.

Seventeen-year-old Jin attended Seoul's Pride parade in 2018. He explained, "I could see many of my friends at the event, and I could meet and be friends with other new people. Also, there were booths around the place so I could get more information about LGBT."

While many older people hold conservative views, the younger generation is far more open-minded. "I came out when I was thirteen, and none of the students from my school took it as a bad thing," Jin said. "And as to my high school experience, I went to an all-boys high school, and the students thought it was interesting. They started talking to me, and it was really good to have people who would listen and be there for me."

Anti-gay protesters continue to show up at Seoul's Pride parade every year, but change is happening in South Korea. "There were lots of protesters near there, and it was really bad, but soon we started making bigger sounds than they made, and it felt really good," Jin told me.

Pride celebrations help make the LGBTQ+ community visible—and that is important in making change! Because most LGBTQ+ people in South Korea are not out, many South Koreans do not know there are LGBTQ+ people in their families and among their friends and colleagues. Once they realize this, they may be more inclined to be supportive. Jin explained that when he first came out, his parents said they didn't understand. But now, four years later, their views have changed and they are more accepting.

And, of course, a visible LGBTQ+ community is important for young LGBTQ+ people and those who are in the process of coming out. Pride lets people know that they are not alone.

"I know there are people still in the closet right now, but I think that going to Pride is a real great thing to do for them even though they feel like they're not brave enough to do it. It felt great to know that I am not the only one and that there are people who I could reach for help. All people at Pride are there for you, for us, for each other...You ain't alone, and you deserve to feel safe, comfortable, and have that sense of belonging."
—Jin, age 17

A rainbow flag flies above the crowds on Pride Day in Seoul, South Korea. Samuel Murray

Mexico City Pride parade.
Marisol Rios Campuzano/Shutterstock.com

MEXICO

Mexico is quite progressive when it comes to LGBTQ+ rights. The country overturned laws that criminalized same-sex relationships in 1871, more than a hundred years before the United States did. National anti-discrimination laws make it illegal to discriminate against sexual minorities, and the government has actively worked to combat homophobia. Mexico City and several states allow same-sex marriage. And although attitudes in smaller towns are often conservative, there are large and colorful Pride celebrations in many Mexican cities every year. The largest of them is hosted by Mexico City. The oldest Pride celebration in the country, it has taken place every June since 1979. The highlight of the event is the Pride parade itself, the Marcha de la Diversidad (March of Diversity).

CELEBRATING PRIDE IN DIFFICULT TIMES

In countries where same-sex relationships are criminalized, where homophobia and transphobia are
widespread and where there is little awareness and
acceptance of LGBTQ+ people, Pride celebrations
can be an important symbol of freedom and hope. So
perhaps it is not surprising that activists in some of
these countries organize Pride events despite the risks.
Where it is possible to hold public events, the media
coverage makes the community more visible, which can
help lead to change. And where it is too dangerous to
organize openly, LGBTQ+ people still come together
to celebrate Pride—even if these celebrations must take
place in secret. Read on to learn about what Pride means
to people in Turkey, Uganda, Russia and Indonesia.

TURKEY

In 2003, Turkey became the first Muslim majority country
to hold a Pride parade. Called Gay Pride Istanbul, it was a
small event, with about thirty people taking part. However,
it was the start of something huge. Every year, more
people attended, and in 2011 the Pride events in Turkey's
capital city, Istanbul, attracted over ten thousand people.

Pride parade in Istanbul's Taksim Square in 2013.
canyalcin/Shutterstock.com

QUEER FACT

IN 2017, LEBANON held its first Pride events. In 2018, the organizer of Beirut Pride—
Hadi Damien—was arrested. He was held overnight at a police station and forced to
cancel the remaining 2018 events. But some events had already taken place: Beirut Pride
opened with a special celebration brunch for parents who support their LGBTQ+ children.

Istanbul's Pride parade in 2013. Two years later the government began banning Pride events.
EvrenKalinbacak /Shutterstock.com

Three years later it was ten times bigger again, with over a hundred thousand attendees. Smaller Pride parades were also held in the Turkish cities of Izmir and Antalya.

Istanbul's Pride march begins in Taksim Square. Participants march the entire length of Istiklal (Independence) Avenue, one of the city's most famous streets. Istiklal Avenue is a wide pedestrian boulevard lined with shops, cafés, art galleries, restaurants, movie theaters, churches, synagogues, mosques and embassies. Many of Istanbul's festivals take place here.

While same-sex relationships have never been criminalized in Turkey, the government has failed to take action to protect LGBTQ+ people. Intolerance and social disapproval are widespread, and violent hate crimes are common. Many LGBTQ+ people in Turkey are forced to hide their sexual orientation to avoid harassment, discrimination or violence. Marchers in the Pride parade carried signs calling for change: *Love knows no gender*; *Another kind of family is possible*; *Stop homophobia*. "In Turkey, we all have difficulty exercising our rights," marcher Aykut Yanak told a reporter. "This is why we must fight and why we all walk together today." Another participant, Senef Cakmak, spoke of the personal meaning the event holds: "Today is the only time of year that I am myself. I don't have to hide from anyone."

After more than a decade of successful and growing Pride events, Pride marches have now come under attack in this increasingly conservative country. The 2015 march

Istanbul Pride parade.
Chris McGrath/Getty Images

> *"I appeal to all governments and societies ... to build a world where no one has to be afraid because of their sexual orientation or gender identity."*
>
> —*UN Secretary-General António Guterres*

Police with dogs stand guard after breaking up a Pride parade in Istanbul in 2018.
Chris McGrath/Getty Images

was banned at the last minute, and the parade was broken up by the police. Since then Pride marches have continued to be banned, with the government expressing concerns about security due to threats of violence from anti-LGBTQ+ groups. Activists have vowed to march anyway, demanding that the government, rather than limiting their freedom, deal with those who are threatening them. Despite the bans, LGBTQ+ people gather in Taksim Square every June, chanting, "Don't be quiet, shout out, gays exist!" Police have broken up these demonstrations by using water cannons, tear gas and rubber bullets, and by arresting both participants and journalists.

"We are not afraid, we are here, we are not going to change," Pride organizers wrote in a public statement. "We painted this street in rainbow for twelve years…showed the beauty of living and marching together to the whole world. We are here again, this time to show we will fight darkness for our pride. We are the ones who declared the revolution of love and gender identity…We are not alone, we are not wrong, and not giving up by any means. Governors, governments, states change, we stay. These threats, bans, pressures will not stop us!"

In 2018, LGBTQ+ people and their supporters came out to march in Istanbul despite the government bans and threats of violence.
Chris McGrath/Getty Images

UGANDA

Same-sex relationships are criminalized in many African countries. In Uganda, the subject was considered taboo until 2009, when a group of American evangelical preachers went to Uganda to attend an anti-gay conference and helped politicians there draft anti-gay legislation. Originally, the bill proposed the death penalty for people involved in same-sex relationships, but this was later reduced to life imprisonment. Under this law, people could go to jail for fourteen years just for knowing someone who was gay and not reporting them to the police.

The public debate about this law provoked anti-gay feelings in an already conservative country. In 2010, a tabloid newspaper called for gays to be executed. It published the names, photographs and home addresses of a hundred individuals it believed to be gay or lesbian,

Uganda's first Pride parade: Cars blasted music; marchers danced, chanted and sang; and children who lived nearby joined in. Rachel Adams

Uganda's first Pride was a weekend-long event. In addition to the march, organizers planned fillm screenings, a fashion show and parties.
Rachel Adams

under the headline *Hang Them*. Three of those individuals—activists David Kato, Kasha Nabagesera and Pepe Julian Onziema—sued the newspaper and won. A few weeks later, David Kato was murdered in his home.

But Uganda's gay and lesbian activists did not give up. Despite the dangers, Kasha Nabagesera and Pepe Julian Onziema continued to fight for LGBTQ+ rights, and both have received international awards for their human rights advocacy.

In 2012, Uganda held its first Pride celebration. More than fifty people gathered for Uganda Beach Pride in a public park on the banks of Lake Victoria in Entebbe, twenty-two miles (thirty-five kilometers) from the capital city, Kampala. Despite police harassment and

"People chanted at the parade: 'We are here! We are here!'... We were telling ourselves that despite the guns that they have pointed square in our chests we are still here, standing, fighting, not moved by the storm."

—Cleo, Ugandan transwoman

In a London, UK, Pride parade, marchers from Rainbows Across Borders (a group that helps LGBTQ+ asylum seekers) show their support for Uganda's LGBTQ+ community.

John Gomez/Shutterstock.com

"This event for me was about celebrating who I am—a transgender person together with my family. I was celebrating courage, strength and solidarity."

—Pepe Julian Onziema, Ugandan LGBT+ activist, transman, Stonewall Hero of the Year 2014

several arrests, the event was considered by the LGBTQ+ community to be a success.

The anti-gay bill was signed into law in February 2014. Gay men and lesbians lost their jobs, were evicted from their apartments and faced increasing violence. A few months later the law was ruled invalid in court— and shortly after that, Ugandans celebrated their third Pride event. This time more than two hundred people took part.

Over the last few years the government of Uganda has become increasingly conservative and hostile to LGBTQ+ people. In 2016, police raided a Pride event, and a number of people were arrested and detained. They were insulted and abused, and some were beaten by the police. The following year, after threats of further violence and with police ready to arrest participants, activists were forced to cancel their Pride celebrations. In 2018, politicians in the country announced their intention to bring back the anti-gay law of 2014. Some activists, fearing for their lives, have been forced to flee their homes and have become refugees (you can read more about this in chapter 5).

In spite of the dangers, LGBTQ+ Ugandans continue to work to educate the public and pave the way for change. And despite the police and government attacks on Pride events, the number of LGBTQ+ activists in Uganda—and the number of people wanting to gather to celebrate—continues to grow.

Marchers chanted "we are here!"—standing up to government officials who had denied that there were gay people in their country. Rachel Adams

MANY OF THE COUNTRIES that criminalize same-sex relationships are former British colonies—which means they used to be ruled by Britain—and their anti-gay laws are in fact very old laws that were passed by the British during the colonial era. This is true in African countries such as Uganda, Nigeria and Gambia; in Asian countries like Bangladesh, Malaysia and Singapore; and in many Caribbean countries as well.

Former British prime minister Theresa May has said she deeply regrets Britain's role in criminalizing same-sex relationships in its former colonies. She asked other leaders to work for change in the thirty-seven Commonwealth countries that still use Britain's anti-gay colonial-era laws. "I am all too aware that these laws were often put in place by my own country," she said. "They were wrong then, and they are wrong now."

Change is happening, and in some cases these old colonial laws are being overturned. In 2016, Belize and the Seychelles decriminalized same-sex relationships, and in 2018, a judge in Trinidad and Tobago found that country's anti-gay laws to be unconstitutional. In India in 2018, the Supreme Court struck down an anti-LGBTQ+ law that had been in place since it was introduced by British colonizers in the 1860s—more than 150 years ago! And during Pride Month in 2019, Botswana's High Court overturned the colonial-era laws that criminalized same-sex relationships.

These successes are giving hope to LGBTQ+ activists in many other countries around the world.

PROUD MOMENTS

KASHA NABAGESERA

Kasha Nabagesera. Martin Ennals Foundation

Growing up as a lesbian in Uganda has meant a lifetime of fighting for Kasha Nabagesera. From the age of seven, she was beaten with a cane for writing love letters to other girls, expelled from numerous schools and forbidden from wearing clothing considered more suitable for boys. At her university, a Wanted poster showed her name and photograph, suggesting she was a criminal. Each class of new students was warned that they could be expelled for associating with her. Kasha was not allowed to live on campus and was forced to sign an agreement stating that she would not go within 110 yards (100 meters) of the girls' hostel.

Despite this brutal treatment, Kasha has always lived openly as a lesbian. The subject was so taboo that for a long time she didn't even know same-sex relationships were illegal. "Every time I got picked on or punished for being a lesbian, I thought they were just using it as an excuse to bully me," she explained. "It's only when I was suspended at university that I took [an] interest in finding out why my sexuality was a big deal for others, and that's when I found out that it was actually illegal to be gay. I did research and found out [that this was true] not only in Uganda and other parts of Africa, but [in other countries] all over the world, and that was my turning point."

In 2003, Kasha founded an LGBTI rights organization called Freedom and Roam Uganda, which she led for the next ten years. Although she was already an accountant, she decided to study human rights law—and began training activists in Uganda and many other African countries. Kasha fought against Uganda's oppressive laws and spoke at numerous international events, raising global awareness of the persecution of Uganda's LGBTI people. She risked her own life by appearing on national television in Uganda, becoming one of the first gay people to openly speak out, and in 2015 she helped launch Uganda's first LGBTI magazine, *Bombastic*.

Kasha has received numerous international awards and honors for her human rights work. In 2011 she became the first LGBTI activist to be awarded the Martin Ennals Award for Human Rights Defenders. Michelle Kagari of Amnesty International said, "Her passion to promote equality and her tireless work to end a despicable climate of fear is an inspiration to LGBT activists the world over."

Many of the early LGBTI activists have had to leave Uganda, but Kasha is determined to stay to support her community. "It's a big sacrifice, but there's no place I really want to live and call home like Uganda," she said. And while life is difficult, she can see that change is happening—and she wants to be a part of it. "I know my children and my grandchildren will not have to go through what I've gone through," she said. "There's a shift in mindset, and that's really something to celebrate."

"Pride is a protest and a celebration to me. A protest to bring attention to the plight of the many challenges faced by the LGBTQI community, and to bring about visibility. And a celebration for the milestones and achievements registered during the struggle for LGBTQIA freedom and equality."
–Kasha Nabagesera

In April 2019, Kasha visited Toronto, ON, to receive an award from the Mark S. Bonham Centre for Sexual Diversity Studies.
Courtesy of Kasha Nabagesera

RUSSIA

Russian LGBTQ+ activists have been fighting to hold Pride parades since 2006. In 2010, the European Court of Human Rights fined Russia for human rights violations, but the Russian government paid the fine and went right on banning Pride events. In 2012, a district court in Moscow issued a ruling banning Pride events for the next hundred years!

Despite these bans, activists have organized Pride parades every year since 2006. These have been held in May, to commemorate the date on which same-sex relationships ceased to be considered a crime in Russia. Each year, Russian LGBTQ+ protesters and supporters from across Europe have marched, and each year they have

Russian activists protest their government's homophobic and oppressive anti-gay laws.
Svetlana Moshkova

been attacked by hundreds of anti-gay protesters who chant homophobic slogans, throw things and even beat and kick participants. Many protesters have been injured by anti-gay extremists, but instead of protecting the marchers, the police have arrested them for participating in the march.

One of the reasons activists have been so determined to hold Pride parades is that they lead to media coverage and make the LGBTQ+ community more visible. And visibility is key to increasing awareness and changing attitudes.

In 2013, the Russian government passed a new law that directly attacked this strategy of visibility, making it more difficult—and more dangerous—for LGBTQ+ activists to fight for their rights. The law banned "propaganda of non-traditional relationships" and was so broadly worded that

Every year, LGBTQ+ people celebrate Pride in Russia despite the risks of doing so. Svetlana Moshkova

A community worker holds a protest sign: *Rainbow flag against fascism!* Svetlana Moshkova

Activists on the streets of Moscow wear colored shirts to create the "Hidden Flag" protest. thehiddenflag.org

any public displays of LGBTQ+ symbols or culture—like holding a rainbow flag—could be considered a crime. This new law has been used to arrest LGBTQ+ activists and protesters. Three activists were fined under this law after they stood in front of schools and libraries holding signs that said *Homosexuality is normal* and *Children have the right to know. Great people are also sometimes gay; gay people also become great.* The three men appealed to the European Court of Human Rights, which ruled in 2017 that the Russian law encouraged homophobia and discrimination and was incompatible with the ideas of equality and tolerance that should be central to a democratic society.

But despite international criticism, Russia's government has shown little concern for the lives of its LGBTQ+ citizens. In 2017, news surfaced that gay men in the Chechen Republic were being rounded up, imprisoned and tortured. Some were killed. An organization called the Russian LGBT Network managed to hide some men in safe houses within the country, and the Canadian government, working with an organization called Rainbow Railroad, managed to help about thirty men escape to safety in

QUEER FACT

IT IS ILLEGAL TO DISPLAY the Pride flag in Russia, but when the World Cup was held there, activists from six different countries found a creative way to stand up for LGBTQ+ rights and show solidarity from around the world. Wearing football shirts from Spain, the Netherlands, Brazil, Mexico, Argentina and Colombia—red, orange, yellow, green, blue and purple—they walked around Moscow as a human Pride flag. They called their project Hidden Flag. Eloi Pierozan Junior was one of the activists who took part. "I come from a very conservative family from a small city in Brazil, so it hasn't always been easy for [me and] my sister, who is also gay. That is why I have been so excited to form part of our unexpected rainbow. I hope it touches the hearts of many people. It's a call to love," he said.

Canada. But the Russian government has taken no action to prevent these horrific human rights abuses.

Despite ongoing oppression and the risk of arrest, Russia's LGBTQ+ community continues to fight for change. And despite bans on Pride events, people continue to seek ways to celebrate their pride. Nikolai Alexeyev, who leads Moscow Pride, has helped activists apply for permits to hold Pride parades in 185 cities and towns all over the country. Over and over again, these events have been denied. In 2018, the government denied permission for a Pride parade to be held north of the Arctic Circle, in the tiny and isolated town of Teriberka. Usually the 2013 law has been given as the reason, but this time the excuse was that the weather would make it too dangerous!

INDONESIA

Indonesia is the largest country in Southeast Asia. Made up of thousands of volcanic islands, it is a beautiful place with mountains and beaches, rain forests and coral reefs. Indonesian society includes people from many different ethnic groups, speaking hundreds of languages. Although the majority of the population is Muslim, the country recognizes six official religions—and the number of religions practiced is much greater than that. The country's national motto is *Bhinneka Tunggal Ika* (Unity in Diversity). Unfortunately, support for diversity does not include an acceptance of LGBTQ+ people.

In recent years, extremist groups have destroyed gay nightclubs and bars, government officials have made public statements condemning homosexuality, and many LGBTQ+ people have been physically attacked and beaten.

"The number of participants was modest compared to Western Prides, and the location was not the beautiful center of the city. But for almost an hour, the International Day Against Homophobia and Transphobia was celebrated under open St. Petersburg skies...As the space for freedoms shrinks around us, the chance to come out in the open and speak out about what's important becomes all the more meaningful for LGBT+ people and for all those who care about justice, equality and humanness in Russia."
—Polina Andrianova of the Russian LGBT+ rights group Coming Out, speaking about IDAHOT 2018

People in Jakarta stand up in support of LGBTQ+ rights on the International Day Against Homophobia, Biphobia, Interphobia and Transphobia.

dani daniar/Shutterstock.com

Two young men in the province of Aceh were publicly caned, and the police attacked and tortured a group of transgender women. Some politicians are pushing for new laws that would criminalize same-sex relationships. For LGBTQ+ people, the climate in the country is hostile—and very dangerous.

It is not yet possible for people in Indonesia to openly celebrate Pride, but a number of LGBTQ+ organizations exist. Although most people must hide their identities, there is still a sense of community. A group called Bali Pride keeps an LGBTQ+ library, and for a number of years the city of Jakarta was host to Asia's largest queer film festival. Sadly, the Q Film Festival was shut down in

QUEER FACT

THE TINY ISLAND NATION of East Timor—officially called the Democratic Republic of Timor Leste—lies just south of Indonesia and north of Australia. East Timor gained independence from Indonesia in 2002, making it Asia's youngest democracy. In 2017, the country held its first Pride parade in the capital city of Dili. The prime minister gave a speech that was posted online. He spoke of his country's long and painful fight for independence and the need to make the most of that independence by accepting and celebrating differences and protecting human rights. "All children need to live in an environment which provides protection, love and the opportunity to develop themselves, regardless of their differences," he said. "As prime minister, I ask you to accept each other, to see each other and have mutual respect."

2017. A few small events are organized every year around Pride or IDAHOBIT (the International Day Against Homophobia, Biphobia, Interphobia and Transphobia, but they are usually cancelled at the last minute due to threats. People still meet in groups to socialize or work for change, but much of this happens out of the public eye, arranged through word of mouth or private texts to protect the safety of all involved. "There is a secret community," activist Eka Nasution told me, "but we cannot express our happiness of being gay."

INTERNATIONAL ACTIVISM

These days the global LGBTQ+ community and its allies are taking full advantage of the possibilities provided by the internet and social media. From Twitter to Instagram, from Tumblr to Reddit, social media is allowing people to come together to talk about what is happening where they live. They share photographs and news articles, and they express—and sometimes argue about—their views. They make connections with others and strategize together. All around the world, letter-writing campaigns build and petitions circulate, challenging discrimination and demanding equality. Money is raised for legal challenges, for public education, for support. Even in the countries with the most oppressive laws, activists make use of the internet to work for change.

"I felt a responsibility to speak up for people who I felt may not feel that they have a voice. I feel like at this time, especially in this political climate, it's really important to speak up for things that really matter to you."

—Adam Rippon, US figure skater, Olympic medalist and first openly gay US athlete to compete at a Winter Olympics

Marchers from all over the world are visible in New York City's Pride March, and many carry signs drawing attention to the need for global activism.
isogood/iStock.com

QUEER FACT

IN 2018, THE WINTER OLYMPIC GAMES were held in South Korea. Activists in Pyeongchang wanted to create a Pride House in the Olympic Village to welcome LGBTQ+ athletes, allies and fans—but they weren't able to get government support or funding. So Canada agreed to host the space as part of Canada House. Pride Houses are an Olympic tradition that began at the 2010 Winter Olympic and Paralympic Games in Vancouver, BC.

Pride march in New York City's Greenwich Village.
a katz/Shutterstock.com

If you want to work toward human rights around the world, you need to know something about the laws that affect LGBTQ+ citizens. The International Lesbian, Gay, Bisexual, Trans and Intersex Association (ILGA)—a worldwide federation with more than a thousand member organizations, representing over a hundred countries—helps with that. It publishes the annual *State-Sponsored Homophobia* report, pulling together the latest research and providing activists, as well as lawyers, judges, journalists and others, with accurate and up-to-date information about the current situation in each country. This report has become an important tool in defending human rights, and you can download it online for free. ILGA also produces a world map of sexual orientation laws.

In 2011, the United Nations launched the Free and Equal Campaign—its first global public education campaign to counter homophobia and transphobia, and fight for legal reforms and equality. Other organizations, like Amnesty International, draw attention to human rights abuses against LGBTQ+ people.

SEEKING SAFETY: LGBTQ+ REFUGEES

For some LGBTQ+ people, life in their own country becomes too dangerous, and they are forced to flee. Many find themselves in neighboring countries that may be little safer than their home country and where finding employment and safe housing can be difficult or even impossible. Some find themselves in refugee camps, where they often face further discrimination and violence. And some are eventually able to resettle in safer countries, where their rights as LGBTQ+ people are protected.

A penguin checks out a Pride flag at Antarctica's first Pride event in 2018.

Aaron Jackson (Planting Peace)

PRIDE CELEBRATIONS have been held in some surprising places. In 2018, Antarctica had its first Pride event—850 miles (1,368 kilometers) from the South Pole in the American McMurdo Station, where hundreds of scientists and researchers stay and work, often for many months at a time. Evan Townsend was one of the organizers of the event—and he managed to take a photo of the Pride flag with the continent's only permanent residents—the penguins! One of the reasons he wanted to hold a Pride event in Antarctica was to show young LGBTQ+ people what is possible. "Having an example of somebody who travels and can have those adventures would've been a great thing for me as a kid but even more so [would have been] being able to see that there are queer people out there who are proud of their queerness and that [it] in no way inhibits them from living these adventures."

PROUD MOMENTS

CELEBRATING PRIDE IN A REFUGEE CAMP

Above and facing page: LGBTQ+ refugees celebrate Pride in a refugee camp in Kakuma, Kenya.
Moses Mbazira, RFK

Located in northwestern Kenya, in East Africa, Kakuma is one of the largest refugee camps in the world. It is home to more than 185,000 refugees. The majority are people who have fled wars in South Sudan, Somalia and other nearby countries—but in 2018, more than two hundred were LGBTQ+ refugees trying to escape the persecution they faced in their own countries. Life in the camp is difficult for everyone, but in addition to the usual hardships, LGBTQ+ refugees face homophobia and transphobia from the local people, other refugees and police. They dream of eventually being resettled in safer countries, but many have been waiting for years. With the United States drastically reducing the number of refugees it accepts each year, it is even harder for them to stay hopeful about the future.

So they do what they can to stand together, look out for each other's safety and fight for their rights. And despite the dangers, on June 15, 2018, they held a Pride celebration. The event included a Pride parade and a talent competition, and hundreds of people attended. People ate food. Some gave speeches. The organizers, who called their group Refugee Flag Kakuma, hoped it would raise awareness and help others in the camp to understand more about LGBTQ+ people.

For the LGBTQ+ refugees, it was a chance to be themselves, to come together and celebrate their brave, diverse and beautiful community. "I am very happy...I feel like I am with my family, and I am very happy for it," said one transgender refugee from Uganda.

It was the world's first Pride celebration to take place in a refugee camp.

> *"I was marching at Kakuma because it was the only opportunity to be who I am, to walk the way I was, to be with people from the LGBTIQ community. I was feeling so proud. I was so happy."*
>
> *—Lwanga Abuson, Ugandan transgender refugee, age 19.*

Moses Mbazira, RFK

Moses Mbazira, RFK

PROUD MOMENTS

FLEEING TO SAFETY

Eka Nasution and Rainer Oktovianus.
enasution.com and raineroktovianus.com

Eka Nasution and Rainer Oktovianus are a married couple who live in Vancouver, BC. Rainer is a photographer; Eka works in health care. Eka likes scuba diving, and Rainer enjoys video games. They enjoy spending time at home together with their cat, Ghost.

But their lives have not always been so peaceful. Both men are from Indonesia, where Rainer was raised in a Christian family and Eka in a Muslim family. In 2010 they met and fell in love.

Except for when they were with close friends, they had to hide their relationship. "There was a total sadness, because I cannot be myself," Eka said. "It was very depressing. There were layers upon layers of fakeness in my life."

Although they kept their relationship a secret, both men spoke up publicly for LGBTQ+ rights, and before long they were targeted by militant homophobic groups. Their photos and address were spread online. They received violent threats and were forced to move more than seven times. "We were always afraid of persecution, of being tortured in public, just because we are gay," Eka said. "When we get threatened, we are afraid to turn to the police, because most of the time the police also persecute us because we are gay."

Fearing for their lives, they turned to a Canadian organization called Rainbow Railroad, which helps LGBTQ+ people facing danger in many countries around the world. With Rainbow Railroad's advice, they were able to obtain visas and make their way to Canada. After they arrived, they applied for refugee status and were accepted. "We had to leave everything behind," Eka said. "We had to leave our country." But there was one important thing they didn't leave: their beloved cat Ghost traveled with them!

In 2016, Eka and Rainer participated in their first Pride parade. They marched with a Vancouver-based organization called Rainbow Refugee, which supports LGBTQ+ refugees from all over the world. "People were cheering— it was like a callout for acceptance, for who we are," Eka said. "When we held that rainbow flag, I thought, This is how it is to feel alive."

"I feel so grateful to be a part of Pride," Eka told me. "It makes me think about how we can pay back the community that has helped us." He and Rainer are definitely doing that. By working and volunteering for organizations like Rainbow Refugee and Foundation of Hope, they are now supporting other LGBTQ+ refugees.

Rainer and Eka sometimes find it hard to believe they are in Canada. "Rainer likes to touch the hedges when we walk," Eka said. "He says, 'I just want to make sure it is all real. That we are really here in Canada, where we can express our identity.'"

"Pride is all about inclusiveness, being brave and fighting for the greater good."
—Rainer and Eka

Eka and Rainer at a Pride parade in Vancouver, BC.
enasution.com and raineroktovianus.com

Pride parade in Thessaloniki, Greece.
Giannis Papanikos/Shutterstock.com

5

YOUNG ACTIVISTS AND THE FUTURE OF PRIDE

LEADING THE WAY

Pride has always been a protest as well as a celebration. Pride is about standing up for LGBTQ+ rights. It is about fighting for freedom and equality. It is about defending the rights of all people to be who they are and to live and love freely and openly. It is about showing the world that queer people are here, that we have always been here, that we are not going away—and that we will not give up.

Young people have been at the forefront of many social justice and human rights movements throughout history, and they are leading the way in the fight for LGBTQ+ equality as well.

Marchers stand up for LGBTQ+ students and safe, inclusive schools at a Pride parade in Portland, OR.
Png Studio Photography/Shutterstock.com

GSAs AND SCHOOL-BASED ACTIVISM

Since the very first high-school-based activism in the early 1970s, LGBTQ+ students and their allies have been working to make their schools safer and more inclusive. Many schools now have GSAs or similar clubs, and these are often started—and run—by students.

In some communities, the kids and teens starting these clubs have had to fight a tough battle. Despite studies that show schools with GSAs have less bullying, some schools have denied students the right to form them. Nevertheless, the clubs are becoming more common and are starting to form in more elementary and middle schools as well as in high schools.

GSAs are open to all students, whether or not they are part of the LGBTQ+ community. Some are large, and

"Activism is being yourself without backing down. It means fighting for yourself and other people. Just showing up and taking pride in ourselves is part of the fight for equality. I love going to Pride because it makes me feel like I belong and that I'm not alone in this fight."

—Micah Cottingham, 16-year-old non-binary activist and artist

Celebrating Pride in Orlando, FL.
Perris Tumbao/Shutterstock.com

others have only a few members. And while some students find them a safe, supportive place to come out, many students join in order to talk about topics like LGBTQ+ history, rights and identities—and to meet other teens who care about social justice. GSAs work toward making their schools safer and more inclusive by creating and putting up posters, holding anti-bullying events and organizing school assemblies to talk about diversity. And many club members also march in Pride parades.

Sixteen-year-old Zoe Steele is co-president of the GSA at her high school in Geneva, Illinois. She identifies as lesbian, or as gay, but she joined the club even before she came out. "The most important thing about having a GSA to me is the sense of community that it provides and the friendships that it helps build," she told me. "I would say if a student is considering joining or starting a GSA,

Members of the Elementary Teachers' Federation of Ontario marched in the 2018 Toronto Pride parade.
Shawn Goldberg/Shutterstock.com

Zoe Steele and her younger sister at a Pride parade in Aurora, Illinois, in 2018. This was the first Pride parade to be held in the city. Laura Steele

just go for it! It's a great way to meet new people and will soon become a safe space to talk and get to know new friends and allies. I think that all schools should have a GSA or a similar group because it is important for everyone to have a place to go for support and friendship."

PRIDE IN THE NORTH: INUVIK'S FIRST PRIDE PARADE

Meet Jasmine and Katelynn, members of a GSA whose work has reached far beyond the walls of their own school. The Aurora GSA is at East Three Secondary School in Inuvik, a town in Canada's Northwest Territories, about 124 miles (200 kilometers) north of the Arctic Circle. Inuvik has a population of just over three thousand people, but the high school draws from a large area, with some students traveling long distances to attend.

The Aurora GSA gave away stickers, buttons and bracelets as part of its Pride celebrations.
Jill Nugent

Aurora GSA students celebrating Pride. From left to right: Kendall Allen, Alyssa Felix, Jasmine Keogak and Katelyn Crocker. Jill Nugent

Eighteen-year-old Inuvialuit student Jasmine Keogak is one of them. Her home community is Sachs Harbour, on Banks Island, a community of just one hundred people located 310 miles (500 kilometers) from Inuvik. Jasmine, who is bisexual and genderfluid, was one of the first students to join the school's GSA—and sixteen-year-old Katelynn Crocker is one of the students who started it.

"I heard a lot of stories from students who weren't being supported in their own schools, so I thought it was important for people to have somewhere to go," Katelynn explained. "GSAs are important for kids who don't have support outside of school."

At first the students organized meetings at their school, put up Safe Space posters and held a wellness day to raise student awareness about the LGBTQ+ community

A car decorated for Inuvik Pride.
Jill Nugent

and the new club. Then they started making bigger plans. "One of the goals since the beginning was to take Pride out of the school and into the community," Katelynn said. But originally they didn't plan to have an actual Pride parade. "It was just going to be a Pride walk with a few people," she said. "The biggest event we'd ever organized was a school bake sale!"

But Jasmine applied for and received a grant to hold a Pride Day celebration, the students met with the town council, and people from the community began stepping up. Katelynn said, "We had people from the hospital offer to put in a float—we weren't expecting that!—and it just kept growing. We had firefighters, RCMP, doctors and nurses from the hospital, the town council, Victim Services…We ended up with so much support. It made me really happy."

Despite the cold temperatures—it was minus eleven degrees Fahrenheit (minus twenty-four degrees Celsius)—about a hundred people showed up to march. "Sparky, the mascot from the fire department, ended up walking at the front with us and racing the kids," Jasmine said, "and everyone had a lot of fun with that."

The day wasn't without challenges. Katelynn explained, "There is a loop that we were planning on walking, but it hadn't been shoveled and it was piled with snow, so we had to walk an extra-long way—like, twice as long—to get back to the school. And it was freezing!"

The students hadn't known what to expect, but when they made it back to the school at the end of the march, they were amazed to see a big crowd already gathered in the gym. "There were close to two hundred people taking part," Katelynn said.

"GSAs provide a safe and welcoming place for students to connect with others like them and find a support system. That was my experience personally! I found that a lot of kids were comforted by knowing that they weren't the only ones when they had a community of people they could see were out—and okay."

—Sandy, age 14

Doctors and nurses from Inuvik's hospital took part in the community's first Pride parade.
Jill Nugent

Trans Pride crosswalk in Lethbridge, Alberta.
Cheers 4 Lethbridge

"We had a barbecue with free food for everyone, and we gave away T-shirts and stickers, and we had musicians performing. People kept coming up and talking to us and congratulating us on how well it was going."

And as for the future of Pride in Inuvik? "I really hope it will be something that happens every year," Katelynn said. "That's what we were trying to do."

RAINBOW CROSSWALKS

Some GSAs have taken their messages beyond their schools in a very visible—and colorful—way: painting those messages on the streets. Many cities, from San Francisco and Miami to Victoria and Charlottetown, have painted rainbow crosswalks as a colorful symbol of Pride. All over Canada and the United States, students are working hard to bring these rainbows to their own communities.

But working for change is often challenging. In some towns, like Springdale, Newfoundland, city councils have refused to grant GSAs permission to paint rainbow crosswalks. The students in Springdale didn't give up, though, and eventually their efforts led to the town's first Pride Week, which included a Pride march and a student-led session on how to be an ally. "When you believe in something and you know it's important to you, it's important to keep fighting for it," said GSA member Claudia Lilly.

QUEER FACT

IN JUNE 2017, ACTIVISTS in the city of Whitehorse, in Canada's Yukon, painted the world's first trans Pride crosswalk in the pink, blue and white stripes of the transgender flag. Just one day later, activists in Lethbridge, Alberta, painted their own—and in August of the same year, Calgary became the third Canadian city to get a trans Pride crosswalk!

In Saskatchewan, students from a middle-school GSA applied to the city for permission to paint Regina's first rainbow crosswalk. They received approval—and got the painting done in time for the city's Pride Week in June 2018.

Troy Fleece/Material republished with the express permission of: Regina Leader-Post, a division of Postmedia Network Inc.

PROUD MOMENTS

Vee Signorelli.
Bre Daoust

BOOKS FOR PRIDE

At age twelve, Vee Signorelli and their older sister started an amazing website called YA Pride. Their website is all about books—in particular, about making sure that LGBTQ+ kids and teens see people like themselves in the books they read.

Books have been an important part of Vee's own coming-out journey. "I am a non-binary trans person, and I use they/them pronouns," Vee explained. "I don't see myself as a man or as a woman. Sometimes I am both, sometimes neither, sometimes some combination of genders."

Vee started to realize they might be trans when they were about fifteen. "It was a really tough process for me, because I'd only seen trans people portrayed as really sad before, and I didn't want to be sad," Vee said. "I also hadn't seen any non-binary people represented, so I didn't know what a future for me would look like. Would anyone actually respect my identity? Use my pronouns? Or would they always think I was a burden? I didn't think that trans people got to have happy endings."

Guess what helped? Books! "Eventually I found some books that featured transgender characters living happy and full lives—and they changed my life," Vee said. "Little by little, I started coming out to my friends, almost all of whom accepted and celebrated me 100 percent."

Vee wanted to help make sure that other teens could find the books they needed. "We all deserve to have access to stories about people like us," they said.

When Vee and their sister started YA Pride back in 2011, there were few books about LGBTQ+ characters, mainly because publishers didn't think people would buy them. "My sister and I knew that was nonsense because we had plenty of friends who wanted to read about queer and trans teens," Vee said. "We wanted to make sure publishing heard one thing loud and clear: there are tons of teenagers who want to buy, read and support LGBTQIA+ books."

They didn't know much about how to run a website, but they were passionate about the cause. They asked authors for guest posts and interviews, and they created an online community that pushed forward the conversation about LGBTQ+ characters. And publishers were listening. "Now," Vee said, "you can hardly keep up with the number of LGBTQIA+ YA books that are being published!"

These days, Vee is a sophomore in college and living in the Twin Cities. "I am an avid bookworm and want to be a writer and teen services librarian when I grow up," Vee said. "For me, pride in my identity has always come from stories, and being able to share that is so important to me."

> *"Pride means rejecting ideas about how you 'should' behave, what you 'should' wear, what you 'should' look like, and fully embracing who you truly are. It takes a lot of courage to do that. To me, pride means having the courage to be yourself."*
> —Vee Signorelli

PROUD MOMENTS

Tru (right) with her brother and sister.
Jenna M. Pullen

TRU WILSON: FIGHTING FOR TRANS KIDS

Pride parades are often led by grand marshals—people who are being recognized for their contributions to the LGBTQ+ community. It is a tremendous honor to be nominated to be a grand marshal—and it happened to Tru Wilson when she was just fourteen.

Tru lives in Vancouver, BC, with her family. Like Harriette, whom you met in chapter 2, Tru is transgender. "As a kid, I always knew who I was. I knew I wasn't a boy, but I didn't have the words to describe it," she said. As Tru got older, she found the words—and when she was nine, she began living as a girl. "At home, at dance, at basketball, I was living as the girl I knew I truly was," she said.

But when her parents informed her Catholic school that Tru was transitioning and wanted to attend school as a girl, the school's administrators refused. They said Tru could not wear the girls' uniform or use the girls' bathroom. "They still used my boy name, and my pronouns, to them, were *he* and *him*," she explained.

Her family moved Tru to the public school system, and they launched a human rights complaint against her former school and the board that governed it—the Catholic Independent Schools of the Vancouver Archdiocese. "We filed a complaint because we didn't want any other child to have to go through the pain I went through," Tru said. Thanks to Tru and her family, the board finally agreed to adopt a new policy, one that accommodates a child's gender expression in school and could include using a student's preferred name, pronoun and uniform.

It was a huge victory—and a North American first—but it was only the beginning of Tru's activism. "Since then," she said, "I've realized that there are so many other kids out there who are having to pretend to be someone they're not in order to please others. So I've become an advocate…I have never stopped living my truth, and that's where I get my power from."

In 2015, at age twelve, Tru was named one of Vancouver's 50 Most Influential People. And in 2017, she and her family were asked to be grand marshals at Vancouver's Pride parade. "I got really excited because Pride means so much to me and so much to everyone. It's just such a great honor. Let's bring on the rainbows—let's go!"

Tru is also an aspiring filmmaker—and an amazing public speaker. You can watch her TEDx talk about her journey on YouTube.

"You are your own person, and you don't have to bend or change because of others' wants of you."
—Tru Wilson, age 14

Tru with her siblings.
Jenna M. Pullen

Tru's family at the Pride parade in Vancouver, BC, where they were grand marshals.
Photo courtesy Michelle Wilson

Pride parade in Brighton, England.
Tristan Fewings/Getty Images

Pride march in New York City's Greenwich Village.
DanielBendjy/iStock.com

HOW YOU CAN HELP

Both locally and globally, there are things that you can do to help. Here are a few (and if you've just read this book, you've already begun the first one on the list!).

- Educate yourself about LGBTQ+ rights. There are some resources at the end of this book that you might find helpful.
- Be an ally. Let your family, friends and teachers know that you support equality for LGBTQ+ people—both where you live and around the world.
- Speak up for equality! Take a stand against discrimination whenever you see it.
- Fight bullying. Challenge anti-gay jokes, comments and stereotypes.
- Join the GSA at your school. If your school doesn't have a GSA, think about taking steps to change that. For information on how to start a GSA at your school,

check out the links in the resources section at the end of this book.

- Use your power as a consumer. Don't give your money to companies that oppose LGBTQ+ rights. Support queer-positive organizations, and watch TV shows and movies that include queer characters—better ratings will lead to more queer content. Buy diverse books or ask your local library to get them. The American Library Association's Rainbow List is a great place to find books with LGBTQ+ characters.

- Write letters to the media and to elected officials, letting them know that you support equal rights for LGBTQ+ people. Sign petitions supporting equality and challenging human rights abuses.

- Organize a fundraiser! Whether it's a bake sale, school dance or something else entirely, fundraisers can raise awareness as well as money. You could donate the proceeds to LGBTQ+ youth groups in your own community, or you could support international groups such as Amnesty and ILGA. If you want to help LGBTQ+ refugees and asylum seekers, an international organization called Rainbow Railroad helps LGBTQ+ people who are facing persecution in their own countries find safety. Rainbow Refugee helps LGBTQ+ refugees resettle in Canada. Or you could support activists who are far away and working for equal rights under difficult circumstances. Even small donations can help groups around the world continue to fight for change.

- And finally, don't forget about Pride Day! Come on out, show your support, and celebrate equality, diversity and freedom with LGBTQ+ people and their allies. Be a part of it!

At a Pride parade in Vienna, Austria. ColorMaker/ Shutterstock.com

Celebrating Pride in Copenhagen, Denmark. Laubelstockphoto/Dreamstime.com

RESOURCES

PRINT

Bongiovanni, Archie, and Tristan Jimerson. *A Quick and Easy Guide to They/Them Pronouns*. Portland, OR: Limerance Press, 2018.

Pitman, Gayle E. *The Stonewall Riots: Coming Out in the Streets.* New York: Abrams Books for Young Readers, 2019.

Pohlen, Jerome. *Gay & Lesbian History for Kids: The Century-Long Struggle for LGBT Rights.* Chicago: Chicago Review Press, 2015.

Prager, Sarah. *Queer. There and Everywhere: 23 People Who Changed the World.* New York: Harper Collins, 2017.

ONLINE

INFORMATION AND SUPPORT FOR LGBTQ+ YOUTH, FAMILIES AND FRIENDS

If you have lots of questions, are looking for good information or need support, **the Trevor Project** is a good place to start: thetrevorproject.org

If you have come out to your parents and they have questions or concerns or want to find a local chapter to meet with, they can contact **PFLAG.** You can also call them yourself for information, resources and support.
PFLAG in Canada: pflagcanada.ca
PFLAG in the US: community.pflag.org

If you are feeling alone, know that there are people who care about you. **It Gets Better** is a website that has recorded videos by more than fifty thousand people from all around the world to tell LGBTQ+ youth—especially those who are feeling alone or dealing with bullying or harassment—that it gets better: itgetsbetter.org

LGBTQ+ RIGHTS

Lambda Legal: This US organization works toward LGBTQ+ equality. Its website has a section for LGBTQ+ youth, designed to help people know their rights and make sure they're respected: lambdalegal.org/know-your-rights

United Nations Free and Equal campaign promotes fair treatment and equal rights for LGBTQ+ people around the world, and its website is a great resource for powerful videos and useful fact sheets: unfe.org/en

ILGA (International Lesbian, Gay, Bisexual, Trans and Intersex Association) publishes an annual report on sexual orientation laws around the world: ilga.org/about-us/annual-reports-documents

GSAs

If your school doesn't have a GSA (Gender and Sexualities Alliance, or Gay-Straight Alliance), you might want to start one. These links have lots of useful information:

Gender and Sexualities Alliance Network (USA): gsanetwork.org

My GSA.ca (Canada): egale.ca/portfolio/mygsa

RESOURCES FOR EDUCATORS

MyGSA.ca: This Canadian website includes a downloadable Equity and Inclusive Education Resource Kit—a guide to starting and maintaining GSAs and other LGBTQ+ student groups or clubs. egale.ca/portfolio/mygsa

GLSEN (Gay, Lesbian & Straight Education Network): This website offers information about GSAs, resources, activities, lesson plans and more, including a jump-start guide for those organizing GSAs and a downloadable Safe Space Kit: A Guide to Supporting Lesbian, Gay, Bisexual and Transgender Students in Your School. glsen.org

SOGI 123: This resource used by schools in BC and Alberta is free and available online for all educators who want to work toward creating schools with LGBTQ+ inclusive policies, climates and curriculum sogieducation.org

The American Library Association's Annual Rainbow List: This is a list of recommended books with LGBTQ+ content, both fiction and nonfiction, for all ages. glbtrt.ala.org/rainbowbooks/rainbow-books-lists

Links to external resources are for personal and/or educational use only and are provided in good faith without any express or implied warranty. There is no guarantee given as to the accuracy or currency of any individual item. Orca Book Publishers provides links as a service to readers. This does not imply any endorsement by Orca Book Publishers of any of the content accessed through these links.

GLOSSARY

ableism—the belief that able-bodied people are normal and people with disabilities are inferior, and the resulting exclusion of and/or discrimination against individuals with disabilities

ally—a person who supports the rights and freedoms of a marginalized or oppressed group that they do not belong to themselves

asexual—a person who is generally not sexually attracted to anyone and feels little or no sexual desire

bisexual (or bi)—a person who is attracted to two or more genders

cisgender—a person whose gender identity matches the sex they were assigned at birth

classism—discrimination against people because of their perceived social or economic class; also refers to the system of beliefs and structures that disadvantages some social classes while unfairly benefiting others

coming out—the process LGBTQ+ people go through as they move toward understanding, accepting and being more open about their gender identity or sexual orientation

discrimination—actions or decisions that treat a person or a group negatively because of their perceived race, sex, age, sexual orientation, gender identity, gender expression, religion or disability

drag—an art form that involves both costume and performance; drag queens are generally men who dress and perform in feminine clothing, and drag kings are generally women who dress and perform in masculine clothing

dyke march—a political demonstration that aims to increase visibility for lesbians and transgender people and all women who love women, however they identify themselves

equality—the state of having the same rights, freedoms, social status, etc.

gay—usually refers to men who are attracted to other men but can also be used more broadly to refer to people who are attracted primarily to people of their own gender. Some women and non-binary people also identify as gay. Gay is also used more generally—for example, to refer to the gay rights movement.

genderfluid—a term used to describe a gender identity that shifts from day to day

gender identity—an internal sense of one's gender (male, female, non-binary)

gender neutral—a person who doesn't identify as either male or female

genderqueer—a person whose gender identity lies outside traditional binary ideas of masculine and feminine; also known as non-binary

GSAs—Gay-Straight Alliances or Gender and Sexualities Alliances, school-based clubs where LGBTQ+ students and allies can meet, support each other and work to make their schools and communities safer and more inclusive

heterosexism—the system of beliefs and attitudes based on the idea that everyone is or should be attracted to the opposite sex, and the resulting prejudice and discrimination against LGBTQ+ people

homophobia—the fear or hatred of people who are gay, lesbian or bisexual

intersex—a person whose physical sex (their body, their chromosomes and their hormones) doesn't fit easily into traditional categories of male or female

labrys—a double-headed ax from ancient Crete, representing lesbian and feminist strength

lambda—a Greek letter used in many countries as a symbol of the gay and lesbian community

lesbian—a woman who is attracted to other women

LGBT—stands for lesbian, gay, bisexual and transgender

LGBTQ+—stands for lesbian, gay, bisexual, transgender and queer; the + indicates the intent to be inclusive of all the identities that make up this diverse community

LGBTQQP2SIA—stands for lesbian, gay, bisexual, transgender, queer, questioning, pansexual, Two-Spirit, intersex and asexual

non-binary—see *genderqueer*

oppression—mistreatment and exploitation of a group of people based on their race, class, sexual orientation, ability, etc.; usually linked to a prevailing belief that the target group is in some way inferior

pansexual—a person attracted to all genders

persecution—the act of treating someone cruelly or unfairly, especially because of race, sexual orientation, gender identity, or religious or political beliefs

queer—a term sometimes used by LGBTQ+ people to refer to all those whose gender identity or sexual orientation falls outside the dominant heterosexual and gender-conforming mainstream

queer-positive—a term used to describe a person, organization or event that supports LGBTQ+ rights

questioning—a term referring to people who may not currently identify as LGBTQ+ but are in the process of exploring and discovering their sexual orientation, gender identity or gender expression

QUILTBAG—an acronym for queer/questioning, undecided, intersex, lesbian, transgender, bisexual, asexual and gay

racism—the system of beliefs and attitudes that holds whiteness to be superior, and the resulting oppression of people of color

repeal—revoke or withdraw officially

sexism—the system of beliefs and attitudes that holds men to be superior, and the resulting oppression of women

sexual orientation—the pattern of a person's romantic and sexual attractions to other people; an individual may be primarily attracted to people of another gender, people of the same gender or people of multiple genders

transgender—term referring to people who do not identify with the gender assigned to them at birth

transitioning—the process of changing one's gender presentation (such as name, pronouns and appearance) to better fit with one's internal sense of gender identity

trans march—a political demonstration that aims to increase visibility, awareness and acceptance of transgender people

transphobia—fear or hatred of transgender people

Two Spirit (2S)—a term used by some Indigenous people to refer to a person who has both a masculine and a feminine spirit; as a broad umbrella term, it can include a wide variety of Indigenous concepts of gender and sexual diversity

REFERENCES

CHAPTER ONE

Apuzzo, Virginia M., and Martha Shelley. "Stonewall Participants." Accessed at pbs.org/wgbh/americanexperience/features/biography/stonewall-participants/

CBC News. "NYC Police Apologize for Stonewall Raid, Catalyst of Modern LGBT Rights Movement." June 6, 2019. cbc.ca/news/world/nyc-stonewall-raid-apology-1.5165304

Cohen, Stephen. *The Gay Liberation Youth Movement in New York: An Army of Lovers Cannot Fail.* New York, NY: Routledge, 2009.

Duberman, Martin. *Stonewall.* New York, NY: Penguin, 1993.

Dunlop, David. "Stormé DeLarverie and Seymour Pine, on Opposite Sides of Stonewall." *New York Times,* June 27, 2016. Accessed at nytimes.com/interactive/projects/cp/obituaries/archives/stonewall-delarverie-pine

Faderman, Lillian. *Odd Girls and Twilight Lovers: A History of Lesbian Life in Twentieth-Century America.* New York, NY: Penguin, 1991.

"The Gay Divide." *The Economist.* October 11, 2014.

Harris, Kathleen. "'Our Collective Shame': Trudeau Delivers Historic Apology to LGBT Canadians." CBC News, November 28, 2017. Accessed at cbc.ca/news/politics/homosexual-offences-exunge-records-1.4422546

Levy, Ron. "How One Man Helped Canadian LGBTQ+ Rights Take Flight." *Huffington Post*, October 10, 2015. Updated October 10, 2016. Accessed at huffingtonpost.ca/ron-levy/canadian-lgbtq-rights_b_8265052.html (A photograph of the "We Demand" document is in the Canadian Lesbian and Gay Archives, accession number 89-038/01.)

Marcus, Eric. *Making Gay History: The Half-Century Fight for Lesbian and Gay Equal Rights.* New York, NY: HarperCollins, 2002.

McCarthy, Justin. "Same-Sex Marriage Support Reaches New High at 55%." Gallup, May 21, 2014. Accessed at gallup.com/poll/169640/sex-marriage-support-reaches-new-high.aspx

Monette, Paul. *Borrowed Time: An AIDS Memoir.* Orlando, FL: Harcourt Brace and Company, 1998.

Pasulka, Nicole. "Ladies in the Streets: Before Stonewall, Transgender Uprising Changed Lives." NPR, May 5, 2015. Accessed August 1, 2018, at npr.org/sections/codeswitch/2015/05/05/404459634/ladies-in-the-streets-before-stonewall-transgender-uprising-changed-lives

Pew Research Center. "Changing Attitudes on Gay Marriage." June 26, 2017. Accessed at pewforum.org/fact-sheet/changing-attitudes-on-gay-marriage

Piette, Alexandria. "In Remembrance of the Stonewall Riots: The Lasting Impact on the LGBTQ+ Community." Accessed August 1, 2018, at womensrepublic.net/in-remembrance-of-the-stonewall-riots-the-lasting-impact-on-the-lgbtq-community

Rivera, Sylvia. "Queens in Exile, the Forgotten Ones." In *GenderQueer: Voices from Beyond the Sexual Binary.* Los Angeles: Alyson Books, 2002.

CHAPTER TWO

Coyote, Ivan E., and Rae Spoon. *Gender Failure*. Vancouver, BC: Arsenal Pulp Press, 2014.

Hernández, Daisy. "Choose Your Words With Cuidado." In *50 Ways to Support Lesbian & Gay Quality: The Complete Guide to Supporting Family, Friends, Neighbors—or Yourself*. Meredith Maran and Angela Watrous, eds. Novato, CA: New World Library, 2005.

Hoad, Neville Wallace, Karen Martin and Graham Reid. *Sex and Politics in South Africa*. Cape Town: Double Storey Books, 2010.

Holliday, Ian. "11-Year-Old Transgender Girl Not Done Yet after Changing Birth Certificate." CTV News, July 23, 2014. Accessed at bc.ctvnews. ca/11-year-old-transgender-girl-not-done-yet-after-changing-birth-certificate-1.1929208

McAfee, Tierney. "Laverne Cox's Heartfelt Message to 'Struggling' Fans: 'Your Stories Matter.'" January 10, 2016. Accessed at people.com/awards/golden-globes-2016-laverne-cox-tells-fans-your-stories-matter

Quinn, Emily. "The Way We Think about Biological Sex is Wrong." Filmed at TEDWomen 2018. Video, 14:06.

Sheldon, Mia, and Jill Krop. "10-Year-Old Transgender Child Fights to Have Gender Removed From Birth Certificate." Global News, December 7, 2013. Accessed at globalnews.ca/news/1008919/10-year-old-transgender-child-fights-to-have-gender-removed-from-birth-certificate

Townsend, Megan. "Anderson Cooper: 'Being Gay Is a Blessing.'" *Glaad*. March 11, 2013. Accessed at glaad.org/blog/anderson-cooper-being-gay-blessing

CHAPTER THREE

Ascah, Adrienne. "Universalist Muslims Embrace Queer Brothers and Sisters." *Daily Xtra*, July 22, 2014. Accessed at dailyxtra.com/ottawa/news/universalist-muslims-embrace-queer-brothers-and-sisters-89649

Baum, Sarah Emily. "Erin Bailey Is Throwing a Pride Festival in Mike Pence's Hometown." *Teen Vogue*, April 13, 2018. Accessed July 31, 2018, at teenvogue.com/story/erin-bailey-is-throwing-a-pride-festival-in-mike-pences-hometown

Brachear, Manya A. "Pride Parade to Put Faith at the Forefront." *Chicago Tribune*, June 24, 2012. Accessed at articles.chicagotribune.com/2012-06-24/news/ct-met-gay-pride-parade-religion-20120624_1_pride-parade-religious-groups-gay-community

Macdonald, Nancy. "Small-Town Steinbach Fills to Bursting with Gay Pride." *Maclean's* magazine, July 12, 2016. Accessed July 31, 2018, at macleans.ca/news/canada/small-town-steinbach-fills-to-bursting-with-gay-pride

Shahla Khan Salter. "We're Queer Muslims and Allies Marching at Pride for Those Who Can't." *Huffington Post*, August 29, 2018. Accessed at huffingtonpost.ca/shahla-khan-salter/lgbtq-muslims-pride-parade__a_23511149

CHAPTER FOUR

Britton, Bianca. "Kasha Nabagesera: The Face of Uganda's LGBT Movement." CNN, March 6, 2017. Accessed at cnn.com/2017/03/05/africa/her-kasha-jacqueline-nabagesera-lgbt-campaigner/index.html

Christie, Bob, dir. *Beyond Gay: The Politics of Pride.* Canada: 2009. 90 min.

Cleo. "Cleo's Moments of Pride." *Bombastic: Our Voices, Our Stories, Our Lives*, 2014. Accessed at issuu.com/bombasticmagazine/docs/bombasticmagazine-electronic

Dougherty, Sarah. "These Are the 6 Openly Gay Athletes Competing at the Sochi Olympics." Global Post, February 5, 2014. Accessed at globalpost.com/dispatch/news/regions/europe/russia/140203/6-openly-gay-athletes-sochi-olympics-russia

Dresden, Hilton. "British PM Theresa May Calls Anti-Gay Commonwealth Laws 'Wrong.'" *Out* magazine, April 17, 2018. Accessed April 21, 2018, at out.com/news-opinion/2018/4/17/british-pm-theresa-may-calls-anti-gay-commonwealth-laws-wrong

Ellifson, Lindsay. "Rippon Says He Had 'Responsibility' to Represent LGBTQ Causes at Olympics." CNN, March 7, 2018. Accessed at cnn.com/2018/03/07/politics/adam-rippon-lgbtq-mike-pence-cnntv/index.html

Free and Equal: United Nations Campaign for LGBT Equality. Accessed at unfe.org/en

The Hidden Flag website: thehiddenflag.org

Jacqueline, Kasha. "The Attack on Gay Rights in Uganda." *Oslo Freedom Forum*, September 28, 2012. Accessed at oslofreedomforum.com/speakers/kasha-jacqueline

"Janet Mock and Jonathan Simkhai Talk International Women's Day, the Oscars, and How to Take Action." *The Standard*, March 8, 2018. Accessed July 26, 2018, at standardhotels.com/culture/jonathan-simkhai-janet-mock-interview

Lavers, Michael K. "US to Ban Uganda Officials for LGBT Rights Abuses." *Washington Blade*, June 19, 2014. Accessed at washingtonblade.com/2014/06/19/u-s-ban-uganda-officials-lgbt-rights-abuses

Miksche, Mike. "Queers Making History at the End of the Earth." *NewNowNext*, May 23, 2018. Accessed August 1, 2018, at newnownext.com/queers-making-history-at-the-end-of-the-earth/05/2018

Okeowo, Alexis. "Gay and Proud in Uganda." *The New Yorker*, August 6, 2012. Accessed at newyorker.com/news-desk/gay-and-proud-in-uganda

Onziema, Pepe Julian. "My Pride Story." *Bombastic: Our Voices, Our Stories, Our Lives*. 2014. Accessed at issuu.com/bombasticmagazine/docs/bombasticmagazine-electronic/67

Power, Shannon. "Timor Leste PM comes out supporting LGBTI rights." *Gay Star News*, July 3, 2017. Accessed August 1, 2018, at gaystarnews.com/article/timor-leste-pm-comes-supporting-lgbti-rights/#gs.tEO3JJg

Rainbow Railroad. "On World Refugee Day June 20, Rainbow Railroad Highlights the Struggles of LGBTQI Refugees and Calls for Governments to Open the Doors for More Queer and Trans Asylum-Seekers." *Cision*, June 18, 2016. Accessed at newswire.ca/news-releases/on-world-refugee-day-june-20-rainbow-railroad-highlights-the-struggles-of-lgbtqi-refugees-and-calls-for-governments-to-open-the-doors-for-more-queer-and-trans-asylum-seekers-685845992.html

"Tens of Thousands Turn Out for Istanbul Gay Pride Parade." *The New Paper*, June 30, 2014. Accessed at tnp.sg/news/tens-thousands-turn-out-istanbul-gay-pride-parade

"This gay soccer league in Mexico is kicking social norms to the curb." *In Circa*, December 1, 2017. Accessed August 1, 2018, at youtube.com/watch?v=Yil5wmb1Vyc

"Thousands March in Seoul for S. Korea's Gay Pride Parade." AFP News, June 28, 2015. Accessed at sg.news.yahoo.com/thousands-march-seoul-koreas-gay-pride-parade-112711794.html

Titi-Fontaine, Sandra. "Gay Rights Activist Calls For End to Hate." swissinfo.ch, October 14, 2011. Accessed at swissinfo.ch/eng/gay-rights-activist-calls-for-end-to-hate/31349340

UN Free & Equal. "The United Nations' Global Campaign against Homophobia and Transphobia." Accessed at unfe.org/about/

Zakharova, Svetlana. "Biggest ever LGBT public demonstration in Russia for IDAHOT." The Idaho Committee. Accessed at dayagainsthomophobia.org/biggest-ever-lgbt-public-demonstration-in-russia-for-idahot

CHAPTER FIVE

"Bring on the Rainbows: Vancouver's Pride Week Kicks Off." *StarMetro Vancouver,* August 1, 2017. Accessed April 5, 2018, at pressreader.com/canada/starmetro-vancouver/20170801/281517931200356

"Newfoundland Town that Nixed Rainbow Crosswalk Hoists Pride Flag for First Time." CBC News, June 4, 2018. Accessed July 31, 2018, at cbc.ca/news/canada/newfoundland-labrador/springdale-hoists-pride-flag-1.4691282

Wilson, Tru. "Living My Truth." TEDxEastVan. Accessed August 25, 2018, at youtube.com/watch?v=Ier2_JqVEWQ

INDEX

*Page numbers in **bold** indicate an image; there may also be text related to the same topic on that page*

ACKNOWLEDGMENTS

The best thing about writing this book is all the wonderful people it has brought into my life. To those of you who helped me write the original Pride book by sharing your thoughts, your stories and your photographs; to those who have generously given me feedback from so many different perspectives; to those who have invited me into their schools and libraries and community centers to talk about Pride; and to those who continue to help get this book into the hands of young readers…you are now far too many to name, but I am so very grateful to every one of you!

This second edition is stronger than the first because of all of you who joined in and allowed your words, stories and photographs to become part of this book. In particular, I am grateful to Alex, Lwanga Abuson, Erin Bailey,

Morgan Brooks, Ryan Brown, Danny Charles, Micah Cottingham, Katelynn Crocker, K.T. Horning, Jin, Jasmine Keogak, Carrie Mac and Esme, Mbazira Moses and Refugee Flag Kakuma, Kasha Nabagesera, Jill Nugent, Eka Nasution and Rainer Octovianus, Emily Quinn, Trystan Angel Reese and Biff Chaplow, Sandy and Shae, Vee Signorelli, Duncan Smith, Zoe Steele, Rachel and Susan Stewart, and Tru Wilson and her family. For stunning photography, thanks to all the talented individuals whose colorful images brought this book to life. For her enthusiasm for the idea of a book about Pride, for being a terrific guide for my first foray into nonfiction and for suggesting—and editing!—this second, expanded edition, I am very grateful to my fabulous editor and friend Sarah Harvey. For all her creativity, enthusiasm and attention to detail, thanks to designer Rachel Page— you made this book so beautiful, not once but twice. And for everyone in the Orca pod, thank you so much for all your support and for always—*always*—having my back. I love working with you and I couldn't be luckier.

Finally, a huge thank-you to my family for their endless love and support. My partner, Cheryl, my son, Kai, and my parents, Ilse and Giles, are always there for me, supporting everything I do and in so many ways. I am incredibly fortunate to be surrounded by such thoughtful, interesting, kind and generous people. So much gratitude and so much love to you all.

People wearing the rainbow flag and the bisexual Pride flag at a Pride celebration in Belgium.

Alexandros Michailidis / Shutterstock.com

A NOTE FROM THE AUTHOR

My first book about Pride was published in 2016. I wrote it because there were no kids' books about Pride, and I thought there should be, but it wasn't until I started hearing from readers that I fully realized how important books like this are. I also had no idea how much that book—and the people I would meet because of it—would change my own life. My experiences and conversations over these past few years have deepened my knowledge of our queer history and strengthened my appreciation for all those who have fought for equal rights over the past half century. They have given me great respect for the younger generation of LGBTQ+ people, who are challenging old ideas and creating new ones. And they have connected me to many wonderful people in Canada, in the United States and in LGBTQ+ communities around the world. I am so grateful for all of this.

It is rare to have an opportunity to expand a book, and I was delighted to have the chance to do so. I love the new stories that I have been able to add and am so grateful to those who shared them with me so that I could share them with readers. While everyone's journey and identity are unique, and no book can include them all, I hope that many kids and teens will see themselves in these pages and feel stronger for this glimpse of a beautiful and brave community.

I also had the chance to update the book—which was surprisingly challenging. When I launched the first edition back in early 2016, I said that the future for LBGTQ+ people had never looked brighter. The political climate has changed since that time, and many people feel less supported, less included, less safe. While actions of governments to roll back human rights have been disheartening, my experiences talking to young people have filled me with hope. Again and again I have been moved by the compassion and sense of justice of the kids and teens I speak with—and by their commitment to create a better, more fair, more inclusive world for everyone. It is important to me that this book reflect both sides of Pride: the celebration of our diverse community and the fierce and ongoing fight for LGBTQ+ rights. In this new edition I have added a chapter with a focus on young activists. I hope their stories will encourage and inspire readers as much as they have encouraged and inspired me.

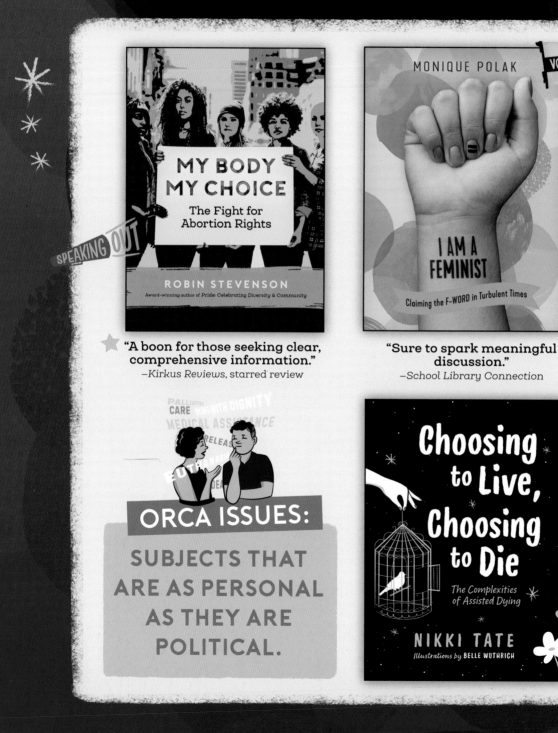